The
Call of God

Jefferson Edwards, Th.M

PNEUMA LIFE

PUBLISHING

THE CALL OF GOD

by Jefferson Edwards

Published by:

PUBLISHING

Printed in the United States of America
2nd Printing

The Call of God
ISBN 1-56229-406-7

Pneuma Life Publishing
P.O. Box 10612
Bakersfield, CA 93389
(805) 837-2113

Contents

Dedication
Acknowledgements
Preface
Introduction

PART I - WHAT IS INVOLVED IN A CALL OF GOD

PART II - THE PROCESSING OF THE CALLED

PART III - THE NEW TESTAMENT PROCESS IN RELATION TO THE OLD TESTAMENT PROCESS

PART IV -   THE PRIESTHOOD-GOD'S FIRST ORDER OF MINISTRY

PART V -   THE CALL TO HIS GLORY AND ANOINTING

DEDICATION

I dedicate this book to the many Timothy's (men) and Timetta's (women) who are pursuing ministry, active in ministry, or advancing in ministry, in whom the Lord has allowed me to impart truth and confirmation to their calls.

I also dedicate this book to the many pastors who I have worked with over the years in confirming and affirming their call of purpose, so that they can continue processing the "Called of God" in their churches.

Finally I dedicate this book to my own sons and daughters in the ministry who I have had personal watch over for their development and release to the Body of Christ.

ACKNOWLEDGEMENTS

I give special acknowledgements to Joan Siebert, my secretary of ten years who transcribed and typed this manuscript over and over during her ten years with me.

Special appreciation also goes to Lois Richardson, our missionary to the Caribbean, who has constantly pressed me to put these teachings in book form. She is a product of these teachings and has taught these principles in many islands in the Caribbean.

Acknowledgements also go to my wife, and co-laborer in the gospel of the Kingdom of God, Debra Edwards. She is the most important living example in my life of the truth of these principles concerning the call of God. She continues to live by these truths and consistently reminds me of the things that she has been taught, and re-imparts these truths in her ministry of confirmation and counsel to me.

Final acknowledgements go to my two daughters, Honesty Joy, and Emiah Meshel, who have given up so much precious time that they could have had with their daddy, to allow me to minister to the Body of Christ at large. They are very much a part of the ministry that the Lord has entrusted me with. Some how through God's purposes, this time will be made up and added to their account in the purposes of God. Thank you darlings for your partnership with daddy in the ministry.

PREFACE

I have participated in a preparatory season where the Holy Spirit has been preparing my segment of the Body of Christ for visitation. I have also participated and have been a catalyst for some islands who have enjoyed a season of visitation of the Lord.

One need that has been common in all these situations is the need to train and prepare ministry for the purposes of God. With most true revivals and times of renewal, come new leaders and potential leaders. I believe that it should be the responsibility of local churches to train their own ministers who reflect the vision of purpose of that local church, island, city or nation.

It is my belief that the Lord sometimes delays visitation because of the lack of prepared vessels for service. I heard God say to me in the latter 1980's, "Jeff, I am ready to visit your segment of the Body of Christ, but they are not ready for Me to visit them. Therefore, you must be involved in a season of 'great preparation' to get your segment ready for My visitation."

One of the main needs that many pastors voice to me is the difficulty that they have in developing teams that work with them in the vision of purpose entrusted to their care. Not only do they voice the difficulty in developing teams, but also in getting a team mentality in potential leaders. This is especially true in the Black neighborhood, where there has been an indoctrination of division. Since 70% of Black families are headed by women, even the family unit does not manifest an atmosphere, that is conducive to developing a unified force or members, that are loyal to a family purpose.

Despite these negative natural intrusions that hinder the development of ministry, there is also the plot of the enemy to destroy a purpose of God in its infancy stage. However, I am compelled to thrust forward and be an instrument of God to develop a new breed of ministry that is well prepared for the times. With this in mind, we present this book to the Body of Christ, recognizing that "preachers are called-but ministers are made. "

- Jefferson Edwards
Kansas City, Missouri - 1993

INTRODUCTION

Some time ago I was returning from Tulsa, Oklahoma, after having ministered to some students there, when the Lord said to me, "Get the ministers ready. I want you to take this message back to the Center and share this teaching with all the ministers there. Teach those who feel they are called of God, those whom God has separated for His service knowing that one day it might be a full-time work." With that command from the Lord, a burden was automatically imparted, which has resulted in the printing of this book.

With that same burden, a workshop was taught to the more than eighty ministers in our assembly. The following is a transcription of the teaching geared toward a ministerial audience. Though at that time were not involved in a formal Bible school as such, we are in the School of Christ.

It is a very serious thing to have the hand of the Lord upon your life and to be used in His service and for His glory! Don't take a call of God lightly. It is a privilege for God to lay His hand upon your life, to use you.

Please realize that if you're called of God it is a full-time commitment, but the Lord may allow you to work in other things which may be full-time as well. Everything that you are doing is **training**. There is nothing you are doing now in which God is not training you. God is able to train you in every area of your life: on your job, in your home, and especially through your family.

If you're called to the ministry, your family is your first congregation! That is where your ministry starts; your home is your first pulpit. It's important to have your family with you spiritually, because they may be the **only** ones who stand behind you in some circumstances, especially in pastoral ministry. So I'm going to deal with some basic principles about ministry, specifically principles concerning the call of God upon your life. Most of these teachings are directed toward those who are already in active ministry or in training for ministry. I have kept the writing informal visualizing a classroom atmosphere, so there will be much use of the word 'you.'

My desire is that you as a minister will become established in some basic principles that stabilize you in ministry, and release you into the full purpose of God.

CHAPTER 1

THE CALL

When God has a calling on your life, many times we do not understand it. Because of our lack of understanding, we are afraid to admit that we are called. But it is only when we will admit, confess, and give way to that call, that we find its effects evidenced in our lives. The call, however, is just the beginning of the process of ministry, and a very shallow beginning in light of the things that are ahead. But to receive a Divine call is a matter of importance!

Do you feel you are called of God to preach? Do you feel you are going to be in full-time service? These are questions that many ministers ponder in their heart until they are established in some concrete principles of ministry.

The basis of a call of God is a Divine encounter with Him. Being called of God does not happen because it's something we want to be, would like to be, or think would be nice. It is based on a Divine encounter with God, when somewhere He intervenes in the affairs of your life and sovereignly calls you to some realm of service. Paul admonished Timothy to realize the implication of this calling. "...who hath saved us, and called us with an holy calling, not according to our works, but according to his own purposes and grace, which was given us in Christ Jesus before the world began" (2 Timothy 1:9).

Once you know you are called to the ministry, you don't need to be afraid of saying it. Be assured in yourself. Be confident that you've heard from God. The Apostle Peter admonishes us to "...give diligence to make your calling and election sure..." (2 Peter 1:10).

Since we know that a Divine calling was necessary for the priesthood of the old order, and since Christ had to be Divinely called, how much more should we be Divinely called? (See Matthew 4 and Hebrews 5) Obviously, you must know that you are called, not by what you think or what you imagine, but with a knowing just as you know that you're born again. It must have that same kind of emphasis and impact! You must have that inner knowing, and it must come from a Holy call resulting from a Divine encounter with God.

It was necessary for the priests of the old order, and it was necessary for Christ, so we conclude that it is necessary for us. Whoever is engaged in the work of the ministry must be assured with inner conviction that he is called of God. If you have not reached the same conclusion, you'll constantly waver and be full of doubts and have misgivings throughout the whole span of your ministry.

THE HUMAN SPHERE
VS.
A DIVINE ENCOUNTER

There are many in the ministry today not because of the election of a presbytery, or the laying on of hands (though I believe in that wholeheartedly), or through asking God to call them into the ministry, but because they are aware that the Lord has called and ordained them. The Apostle Paul said, "But when it pleased God, who separated me from my mother's womb, and called me by his grace. To reveal His Son in me, that I might preach him among the heathen: immediately I conferred not with flesh and blood:" (Gal. 1:15-16). Whatever man does is always secondary to what God does. Your call must not be based on anything another person says; it must be based upon a Divine encounter with God. That is first and foremost, and then the human agency comes into play.

When God ordained King Saul through the prophet Samuel, it was obviously God's calling, but the people agreed with what God had done (See 1 Sam. 10:1,24). The same thing was true with David, God ordained, and the people received what God had done (See 1 Sam. 16:1,13; 2 Sam. 2:4; 5:3). The basis of the call must be God, and the human encounter must be subservient to the Divine encounter. You must not be in the ministry as a result of a human call; it must be based upon God's dealings with you. That is why when one professes a call to preach, it has to be between him and the Lord.

When it is God's time, He will confirm your call in the church. If your call to the ministry is based on anything other than a Divine encounter with God, even if you've had a prophetic Word from someone, you'll be in trouble when the going gets tough. For then you'll say, "But Pastor said..." and Pastor is not going to have any power to hold you up. Only God can sustain you, so the call must be based upon Him. Paul expresses his assurance of who had called him this way; "Being confident of this very thing that **He** which hath begun a good work in you will perform it until the day of Jesus Christ" (Phil. 1:6). And again He put it this way; "...For I know whom I have believed and am persuaded that He is able to keep that which I have committed unto Him against that day" (2 Tim. 1:12).

NOTES

CHAPTER 2

THE CALL OF JEREMIAH, THE PROPHET

Let's start at Jeremiah, Chapter 1, and we will look at the call and the touch of God as it concerned Jeremiah and as it relates to us today.

"Then the Word of the Lord came unto me saying, Before I formed thee in the belly I knew thee: and before thou camest forth out of the womb I sanctified thee, and I ordained thee a prophet unto the nations" (Jer. 1:4).

If God has a call on your life for some specific area of ministry, it just didn't happen out of a spontaneous impulse. It was a part of His plan, even before you were born. All your life, even those things you did before you knew the Lord, all those things were leading up to this end, that God might bring you forth for the ministry to which He has called you. All those things were training and preparation. Understand that God does not call people who are saints already.

Once you are called, there is an **anointing resident with that call** even without being filled with the Holy Spirit. There are many ministers that are not filled with the Holy Spirit, but they have an anointing as a result of the call of God on their lives (See Acts 18:24-28). God wants them to have enablement that comes with the call; however, to continue on in the process of God and in the baptism of the Holy Spirit, a matter of the will and choice of the minister is involved (See Acts 5:32). Most of the time the anointing is resident **for you**, to deal **with you** and to **change you**!

The anointing may not manifest itself in outward works initially, but there is an anointing that is resident with the call! In going back over your life, you should be able to see how God was preparing you to bring you into ministry. Of course, there are some things you don't see now, but eventually you will see God in them. From the very first cry that came out of your mother's womb, from the very first step you took, you were being shaped for service. This same truth is evidenced in Jeremiah's call. "Before I formed thee in the belly I knew thee: and before thou camest forth out of the womb I sanctified thee, and I ordained thee a prophet unto the nations. Then said I, Ah, Lord God! Behold I cannot speak: for I am a child" (Jer. 1:5-6).

I think we would all agree that when God calls us, we have plenty of excuses why we can't follow. In my own life, when I knew I was called to the ministry, I fought it for three days. It came out of the blue. As far as I was concerned, I wasn't doing anything spiritual. I wasn't looking for God, I wasn't even thinking about God. I was doing my own thing, and I was going at it pretty good. Once He called me; however, I just couldn't understand or see why in the world the Lord would want to use me. There was no way to explain it and that blew my mind. I kept asking "Why me?" For three days I didn't eat a thing and I had to get away. This might not be a pattern for you, it's just a personal expression of what I went through.

Finally, through Isaiah the first chapter, the Lord began to speak to me, "Listen, let us reason together. The dumb ox knows his master. You are supposed to be so intelligent and you don't even know who your master is. You call an ox 'dumb,' but he knows his master; the one who feeds him and takes care of him. You can't reason with Me, even though I'm reasonable; you can't reason out My purpose and My plan. You either accept the fact that I called you, or you are going to keep going on for years wondering why I would call you."

If you continue in that mentality, you will never accept your call, because usually there are not many recognizable qualifications at first. Many times a person doesn't understand why. They run around trying to find out why God would call them. They haven't come to the point where they can say, "Okay, Lord, I accept the call."

When God calls you, everything you need to fulfill that call is resident within the call. You can look at yourself and say, "No, I can't do it." And that is actually true. If you think you can't do it, you've got a long way to go. You're going to have a real "breaking-down" process. When God calls us we are not qualified, so it's perfectly normal to say, "Why me, Lord?" You are looking at and evaluating yourself. Of course, you are not ready, You can't be used now in the full expression of the call, but the basis of the call is not upon what you are now. It is based upon what He's going to make you to be if you accept the call. Paul declared, "But by the grace of God I am what I am..." (1 Cor. 15:10), and again "Whereof I was **made** a minister, according to the gift of the grace of God given unto me by the **effectual** *(operative, active)* working of His power" (Eph. 3:7).

You look at yourself and you see nothing that qualifies you for ministry; not one thing, so you can't evaluate yourself now, and you can't put a time period on God. The process can be quick and you can move forth in the ministry to which God has called you, or it can be very long. It depends upon you!

Basically, it depends upon how much you are willing to yield to God's dealings. How much are you willing to give yourself to God's ways and give yourself to the Word of God? **"Let the Word of God dwell in you richly in all Wisdom..."** (Col. 3:16). When he says **richly**, that means to its highest realm.

JEREMIAH - A DIVINE ENCOUNTER AND A DIVINE TOUCH

"But the Lord said unto me, Say not, I am a child: for thou shalt go to all that I shalt send thee, and whatsoever I command thee thou shalt speak. Be not afraid of their faces: for I am with thee to deliver thee, saith the Lord" (Jer. 1:7-8). All of us have excuses: "I can't speak before a crowd. I can't talk to strangers. I can't. I can't." Yes, that's true. Many people are stifled in accepting the call of God because of these inabilities which are magnified the more they look at themselves. In looking just at themselves, they stay in that mentality of 'I can't.' When you look at yourself you will see nothing but failure and insufficiency. "Not that we are sufficient of ourselves to think anything as of ourselves; but our sufficiency is of God" (2 Cor. 3:5).

"Then the Lord put forth his hand, and touched my mouth..." (Jer. 1:9). Not only must it be a divine encounter with your call, but it must be a divine touch from God. There must be a divine touch upon your life. God has got to touch you! When it comes to the anointing of a call, there is a touch involved. This involves a closeness and an active relationship. The anointing is not a distant thing; it's something that comes as a result of being close and involved. The call and the anointing must be the result of a relationship with God. As a result there will be a touch of God upon your life.

The touch can be compared with the material used in construction of the Tabernacle of Moses. There was shittim wood *(flesh)* overlaid with gold *(Divinity)* (See Exodus 25). That's all that we are, shittim wood, but God overlays us with gold. Though He does not take away the wood, the wood begins to manifest itself in His character, in His nature and in His way.

"Then the Lord put forth His hand, and touched my mouth. And the Lord said unto me, Behold, I have put My words in thy mouth" (Jer. 1:9). He has to give you something, because you don't have it to begin with. "See, I have this day set thee over the nations and over the kingdoms, to root out, and to pull down, and to destroy and to throw down, to build, and to plant. Moreover the word of the Lord came unto me, saying, Jeremiah, what seest thou? And I said, I see a rod of an almond tree, Then said the Lord unto me, Thou hast well **seen**; for I will hasten my word to perform it" (Jer. 1:10-12). You will see all this in this passage of Scripture. There must be a call that comes as a result of a divine encounter, and then there must be a touch from God.

This touch must bring forth a change in our lives. It should cause us to see things different because the touch of God will change our eyesight, even as the Lord changed the eyesight of Paul (See Acts 9:8-9). The religious leaders of that day knew that Peter and John had been with Jesus (See Acts 4:13).

Many times in Scripture when God touched someone they received strength, courage, wisdom, or direction. Looking at the life of Daniel, the prophet, we see five distinct times where the Lord touched him and there was change which resulted from that touch. In Daniel 8:15-19, he received a touch from God in which he received "vision," "sight," and "understanding." In Daniel 9:20-22, he received a touch from God that resulted in him receiving "skill" and "teaching." In Daniel 10:9-11, he received a touch from God which caused him to "stand up." In Daniel 10:15-16, he received a touch from God in which he was able to "speak." And finally, in Daniel 10:17-19, he received a touch from God which imparted to him "strength."

So when we are touched by God, our present state and condition is changed, and we receive something from the Lord to enable us in what we are called to be and to do.

JEREMIAH - THE COMMISSION AND VISION

The next thing is that there must be a commission or a vision. In Jeremiah 1:10-19, He told Jeremiah what **He was going to do** and then Jeremiah **saw** something! What really starts a call into action is a glimpse of what the call is going to bring you to. I can say honestly within my own life I see a lot that is afar off, but I don't see how to get there. I see the end, but I don't see the means. God gives you some aspect of ministry which may be temporary, but there is also a long range commission.

I am reminded of when the Lord appeared in a vision to Samuel when he was a boy. First he appeared to him and then later on He gave him something **to do**! He told him: "Here is what I want you **to do**." Now I don't think that is all of his ministry, but He gave him some incentive to move forward. There must be a vision, a commission given, and if it's not a specific vision or a personal vision, He'll hook you up with somebody that's got a vision. There must be something given which leads you toward what He wants you **to be** and **do** or you will have no direction or incentive to move forward. The Lord wants you to begin to move toward the call as a result of what He shows you.

In Scripture, for everyone that was called of God, not only was there a Divine encounter **with the call**, He also **touched** them, and at the same time He **commissioned** them. In Scripture they were always **commissioned** or given some glimpse of what they were **to do**. It is important to understand this particular principle involved in ministry (See Isa. 6:9; Gen. 12:1-3; Ex. 3:7-10; Josh. 1:1-9; Judges 3:20; 6:14,25-26; Ezek. 3; Hosea 1:2; Matt. 28:19; Acts 9:6, 15-16). If God is now beginning to show you what He has for you to do, that's good. After the call, it is important to get into a position where God can speak to you as a result of your call. Sometimes the reason why the Lord doesn't talk is because we run with the call and don't wait on the commission.

There must be a commission with the call because the call is a result of something specific in the mind of God. God doesn't just call you to be calling you. A lot of folks say that they are called, but for what? God doesn't play around. He's very orderly. If God has called you, it's for a specific reason. He has something for you to do. So, there is a commission given.

I am not saying that you will automatically understand every aspect of a given commission, because the Lord gives progressive revelation and understanding. But you will know that God's given you something to do, though you may not be able to explain it in its entirety at the beginning. This is illustrated in Paul's life — "And he trembling and astonished said, Lord what wilt thou have me to do? And, the Lord said unto him, **Arise** and go into the city, and it shall be told thee what thou must do" (Acts 9:6). As Paul was obedient to the command from the Lord to:

"...Arise, and go...", then the Lord was faithful to send Ananias, who gave Paul more understanding. "...He is a

chosen vessel unto Me, to bear My name before the Gentiles, and kings, and the children of Israel..."
(Acts 9:15).

Paul did not understand all the implications of this commission at that time. For years I couldn't explain anything God spoke to me though I knew it inside, but at the same time there was a knowing and the knowledge of that commission began to progressively increase until I found words to begin to express it. As a result of a **call** and a **Divine** encounter and touch from God, you should be understanding the commission He has given you more and more!

He told Jeremiah what He had sent him to do, and then He showed him a vision to move toward it. God said, "What do you see? I'm going to perform it." The Word of the Lord came unto Jeremiah and God told him **to do** something!

"And the Word of the Lord came unto me the second time, saying, What seest thou? And I said, I see a seething pot; and the face thereof is toward the north. Then the Lord said unto me, Out of the north an evil shall break forth upon all the inhabitants of the land" (Jer. 1:13-14). Since Jeremiah was called to be a prophet to the nations, he started having revelation of things concerning the nations. As a result of a call, you can expect revelation to begin to flow in line with that call. You are going to be able to see things that are consistent with that call and that commission if you walk in progressive obedience to what the Lord says. Your obedience to the call will trigger the spirit of revelation.

For instance, if you know that one day you are going to pastor a church, you're going to begin to see people like you've never seen them before. The call is going to trigger revelation.

It is going to open the door for you to begin to see how the shepherd must love the sheep. The call is going to cause you to be dealt with so that you can move in the realm of love that is required of a pastor. That is true for any ministry.

The call is going to cause you to become more sensitive to the things of God so you can be more sensitive to the things concerning people. Your dreams and your visions will begin to correspond with the call. From the day of a divine encounter, a divine touch and a commission, you should be constantly **seeing** what God has for you in everything that concerns your life.

Look for God in that which concerns your life. You can be on your job working, no matter what you work with. God is speaking to you even through that. Your mentality should be, "Now, see I have to do this work just right, because I'm working for this guy right here. If I don't do this just right, it is going to come back to me, and they are going to find out that I messed it up. Someone could get a bad product and I don't want that to happen. It would bring a bad name to the Lord since I represent Him on this job. That is why I must make sure that I keep right with the Lord because whatever I produce, I want it to be fruitful to the people." Learning to be careful and concerned about what you do in the natural, in relation to your employer, works integrity and responsibility in you, to be useful in God's service (See 1 Tim. 3:7).

In Genesis 1:11-12, a principle is established that we produce seed after our own kind. There are some things you have become, that you know God has worked in you and you would like others to receive the seed of that work. But there are some other things in you that you don't want others to receive. You produce seed after your own kind. Sometimes we see things we don't like about ourselves in our children. You produce seed after your own kind. That is not only in the human sphere, but it is in spiritual things as well. There is a seed of being late, but you must become aware of that bad seed and begin to work on that lateness. You shouldn't want that kind of seed sprinkled in the congregation; if it is in the leadership it will be in the congregation also.

Some things you do not want reproduced, but in the ministry God has given you, you'll find that more of what you do is creative; it is reflected and people receive it. They look at you being in leadership before they see anyone else, and it is easy for people to receive your seed. Your wives can reflect the bitterness you have. They are near you and they can pick up your seed. Also, wives, your husbands can do the same thing. That is why we must stay in God's presence and be conscious of His presence continually and keep pure. I want my seed to go out and be good because the seed does mingle with you, even the seed of the Word. God meant for the Word to become flesh in you and go out. What He has given you, what He has enabled you with **must** become flesh in you, and then flesh in others.

So the Lord says, "out of the north.." to Jeremiah. Revelation began to trigger. He began to speak to him concerning his call because He had called him concerning the nations. So what did He begin to speak with him about? The nations! He began to speak to Jeremiah about the nations because He said, "I called you not only to Judah and Israel, but other nations." Elijah went and anointed one man to be king over Syria (See 1 Kings 19:15; also, Amos 1:-2). When Jeremiah was called, his commission was to be over the nations, so God began to speak to him about the nations. "And out of the north he shall break forth upon the inhabitants of the land. For, lo, I will call all the families of the kingdoms of the north, saith the Lord; and they shall come, and they shall set every one his throne at the entering of the gates of Jerusalem, and against all the walls thereof round about, and against them touching all their wickedness, who have forsaken me, and have burned incense unto other gods, and worshipped the works of their own hands" (Jer. 1:14-16).

His commission was broad, and God's commission to you will be broad, but the more you begin to give in to that call and give into that touch of God on your life, and that commission, the more specific God will begin to speak to you. God said, "You're over the nations." That is a broad call, a broad commission. Nevertheless, it is a commission. You need to receive the principle that the commission is progressive. If you're not going to receive the commission in its broad application, there is no sense in God telling you any specifics. You must understand this in order to grow and progress in the call. When you finally say, "Okay, Lord, I accept it," God begins to move and show you more.

Proverbs 4:7 says, "Wisdom is the principle thing; therefore get wisdom: and with all thy getting get understanding." Once you **accept** the overall wisdom of God, though it may be broad in scope and expression, then God is able to give you understanding, line upon line, precept upon precept (See Isa. 28:9-10). More and more that commission should become specifically related to what He has called you to do. You should begin to grasp and yield to more of what God has said to you, seeing it in more detail as you progress. You may have a broad commission, but it begins to tune in to your life in the Lord's timing, and the understanding becomes greater.

How do we understand? By faith (See Heb. 11:3). We believe what He has said, because faith cometh by hearing and hearing by the Word of God (See Rom. 10:17). Evidently Jeremiah believed that he was called over the nations. That was a door and he accepted it; he just went through one more step. God **called** him! That's like one step. At one level he accepted the commission, then he stepped up to another level and God was able to speak to him again and take him up to other levels of expression of the commission.

There are progressive steps and you can miss some of them. If you miss some steps, you have to start over where you left off. You can't skip the steps and get to greater levels of expression of the call. There are progressive steps toward the fulfillment of your calling. So the Lord began to speak to Jeremiah specifically, "Thou therefore gird up thy loins, and arise, and speak unto them all that I command thee: be not dismayed at their faces, lest I confound thee before them. For, behold, I have made thee this day a defenced city..." (Jer. 1:17). That means no one is going to touch you or harm you; I'm going to be with you. Don't be afraid. But sometimes God tells us something and we say, "On no, I can't do that; I'll get killed." Then we get unbalanced in our emotions and we don't listen to Him tell us about the rest of it.

There is no reason for you to be afraid. God said, "I'm going to make you a defenced city, and an iron pillar, and brazen walls against the whole land..." That means that no one in the whole land is going to destroy you and that goes along with the commission given to Jeremiah, "against the kings of Judah, against the princes thereof, against the people of the land. And they shall fight against thee (*I want you to know that*), but they **shall not** prevail against thee; for I am with thee, saith the LORD, to deliver thee'" (Jer. 1:18b,19). Now all of those promises were involved in a **divine call**, a **divine touch**, and a **divine**

commission and **vision**! Every Scripture in that chapter was involved in a divine encounter and a **call** to ministry, but remember, the call was progressive and had within it the capacity to increase and elevate as Jeremiah was obedient and responsive.

NOTES

CHAPTER 3

ISAIAH - REMOVAL OF THE CRUTCH

"In the year that king Uzziah died.." Uzziah was a king who did that which was right in the sight of God. The prophet Zechariah was around him, and as long as he was there, he kept Uzziah balanced. God granted him favor, but Uzziah got lifted up, and went into the temple of the Lord to burn incense upon the altar of incense, and tried to offer sacrifice himself. He went beyond what he was supposed to do, and was stricken with leprosy. Then his son Jotham reigned in his stead, even while he was alive, because he had to stay in a separate house. The lepers could not come among the normal people. He went in the temple and the priest said, "You know you are not supposed to be in here." He got mad at them, but they were just doing what they had to do. While he was angry, leprosy began to appear on his forehead (See 2 Chronicles 26).

Uzziah was Isaiah's uncle and most people preach that he was a real crutch for Isaiah. If your uncle is a king, in many ways, you've got it made. Lots of things can be crutches. That's why sometimes there is even a separation in your own family. Though you're together physically, God separates you spiritually and sometimes physically too. He may spiritually separate husbands and wives (See Mt. 10:32-38). Even though they are called to a ministry together, each one has to accept the call individually (See Rom. 14:12).

A wife cannot accept the call of ministry in her husband's life. She has to accept her own call in line with his. Even though they are called together, she has to accept the call that her husband might have. Now your wife is called if you are called, but she does not have to accept the call. It is still dependent upon you, personally, to accept the call, and her, personally, to accept the call, or vice versa. Sometimes God has to deal with one partner by himself, in order to get both together. You cannot make your wife or husband accept your call. We see that principle acted out in Abraham's call in Genesis 12:1, and in the life of Jesus (See Luke 4:16-32; Mt. 13:53-58).

Many times the people we are close to, hold us in certain categories and will not encourage or accept the change that has come to our lives as a result of being called. These are people we have depended upon for our livelihood. But when you are called by God, He must become your livelihood. Paul said, "For in Him we live, and move, and have our being..." (Acts 17:28).

Abraham had to come out from under the influence of his father that worshiped idols. Abraham had to be totally dependent upon the Lord in order to allow the training process to begin, to come to relationship with the Lord and levels of expression of his call.

We must be yielded to the hand of the Lord without restraint or reservation, if we are to become what the Lord has called us to be. That's why we must bring the Lord and what He has called us to do to a level of top priority above **every** other relationship (See Luke 14:26-27,33; Luke 9:57-62).

ISAIAH - DIVINE ENCOUNTER, TOUCH AND COMMISSION

"In the year that king Uzziah died I saw also the Lord sitting upon a throne, high and lifted up, and his train filled the temple. Above it stood the seraphims, each one had six wings; with twain he covered his face, and with twain he covered his feet, and with twain he did fly. And one cried unto another, and said, Holy, holy, holy, is the Lord of hosts: the whole earth is full of his glory. And the posts of the door moved at the voice of him that cried, and the house was filled with smoke. Then said I, Woe is me! For I am undone; because I am a man of unclean lips, and I dwell in the midst of a people of unclean lips: for mine eyes have seen the King, the Lord of hosts. Then flew one of the seraphims unto me, having a live coal in his hand, which he had taken with the tongs from off the altar. And he laid it upon my mouth, and said, Lo, this hath touched thy lips; and thine iniquity is taken away, and thy sin purged. Also I heard the voice of the Lord, saying, Whom shall I send, and who will go for us? Then said I, Here am I; send me. And he said, Go, and tell this people, Hear ye indeed, but understand not; and see ye indeed, but perceive not. Make the heart of this people fat, and make their ears heavy, and shut their eyes; lest they see with their eyes, and hear with their ears, and understand with their heart, and be converted, and be healed. Then said I, Lord, how long? And he answered, Until the cities be wasted without inhabitant, and the houses without man, and the land be utterly desolate, And the Lord have removed men far away, and there be a great forsaking in the midst of the land. But yet in it shall be a tenth, and it shall return, and shall be eaten: as a teil tree, and as an oak, whose substance is in them, when they cast their leaves: so the holy seed shall be the substance thereof."

(Isaiah Chapter 6)

In this account of the Prophet Isaiah's call, the same principles are seen as was in Jeremiah's call. Isaiah had a vision of the Lord and this involved a **Divine** encounter. In verse 7, he was **touched** by one of the seraphims upon the mouth. A touch was involved with this Divine calling. In verse 9, the Lord told Isaiah to "...Go and tell this people...," which was a **commission** given. Then in verse 11, the Lord even gave the extent of the commission, again a **Divine Encounter**, a **touch**, and a **commission**.

Notice that when Isaiah was touched by the LORD, there was a change in his nature and in his state. As a result, he was in a position to hear the LORD and receive a commission from Him. The Divine **encounter**, **touch**, and **commission** all happened at the same time.

Sometimes these elements are progressive; basically, because the Divine **touch** has to bring a change of state in order to receive or be in a position to hear God clearly and be commissioned. Then, too, there is no progression if the call is not accepted.

It's important that you be changed to some degree by the touch of God upon your life and continue to allow His Divine touch to permeate your being. To the measure you are changed in giving in to His touch, in that same measure you are exalted to a level of expression in the commission He gives (See 1 Peter 5:6; James 4:10).

CHAPTER 4

SAMUEL - HIS CALL AND COMMISSION

"And the child Samuel ministered unto the Lord before Eli. And the word of the Lord was precious in those days: there was no open vision. And it came to pass at that time, when Eli was laid down in his place, and his eyes began to wax dim, that he could not see; And ere the lamp of God went out in the temple of the Lord, where the ark of God was..." (I Samuel 3:1-3).

The lamp of God almost went out in the temple of the Lord. Eli had come to the place where the lamps were not kept right under his administration. There was almost no witness of the Holy Spirit, nor light of the Word. A lamp always speaks of the witness of the Spirit or the presence of God and the Word of God! The Holy Spirit always comes to show you what will be. He always comes that we might see! Where the altar of God was, you couldn't see the presence and witness of the Lord anymore. The lamp was almost out! They didn't recognize the presence of the Lord nor could they see or eat the bread (*fellowship*) at the table because the lamp was almost out!

"...The Lord called Samuel: and he answered Here am I. And he ran unto Eli, and said, Here am I; for thou callest me. And he said, I called not, lie down again. And he went and lay down. And the Lord called yet again, Samuel. And Samuel arose and went to Eli, and said, Here am I; for thou didst call me. And he answered, I called not, my son; lie down again. Now Samuel did not yet know the Lord, neither was the Word of the Lord yet revealed unto him" (Verses 4-7). Even though he was involved in the service of the house of the Lord, he did not know the Lord. It is possible to be around the house and still not know Him!

"And the Lord called Samuel again, the third time. And he arose and went to Eli, and said, Here am I, for thou didst call me..." (Verse 8). Notice how God is persistent about a call. He will keep calling, though some folks will never answer. He never stops calling you if you're really called, but it is still up to you to answer. He won't force you; there has to be a personal acceptance!

"...And Eli perceived that the Lord had called the child. Therefore Eli said unto Samuel, **Go**, lie down: and it shall be, if he call thee, that thou shalt say, Speak, Lord; for thy servant heareth. So Samuel went and lay down in his place. And the Lord came, and stood as at other times..." (Verses 8-10). It was the Lord Himself that came and called. Samuel may not have seen anything, but the Lord was there. Here Samuel had a Divine encounter. "...Then Samuel answered, Speak; for thy servant heareth. And the Lord **said** to Samuel, Behold, I will do a thing in Israel, at which both the ears of every one that heareth it shall tingle. In that day I will perform against Eli all things which I have spoken concerning his house: when I begin I will also make an end. For I have told him that I will judge his house forever for the iniquity which he knoweth; because his sons made themselves vile, and **he restrained them not**" (Verses 1-13).

With a call, it is important for you to **obey** God in the things that concern your family. Now your responsibility is to tell them what God says and if they don't yield after you tell them *(because you can't make them yield)* then the effects of not yielding is upon them. God said about Abraham, because he's a friend of mine and I know that he will command his family and his children and his household to walk in the statutes and the precepts of the Lord, that I might fulfill all that I have said to him (Genesis 18:19, paraphrased).

In 1 Timothy 3:4, the principle is clearly seen that your family is your first congregation. The LORD said, "I know Abraham will command his family!" If **you** will **be faithful to obey God, He will get your family together**! He WILL! He is faithful! God is ready to deal with all disobedience, when your obedience is fulfilled (See 2 Corinthians 10:6).

I know one brother who kept saying over and over again to me, 'But my wife,...my wife...but my wife. I'm waiting for my wife.' I told him that we don't walk by sight, we walk by faith! What you are saying is, "Lord, before I move into what You have called me to do, I want to see You change my wife and deal with her." God doesn't move by sight. He moves by faith and so should we. I said, "Why should God get your family together, when you are not doing what He has told you to do? You're not in any position for God to give you His favor in your family. You are not in any position for God to bring anything to your family because you are not obeying Him yourself!" You can sit there and use the excuse of 'my wife or my husband' for a long time and you will be going in a circle.

You will never progress in ministry. Nothing can hinder a call of God, if you will yield to that call. He's going to see the family through! He's going to work in that family, and work out that family situation.

When I was called to the ministry, the first opposition was my loved ones; they almost turned me back several times. That was my worst enemy. One of the first visions I had after my call, was that the enemy was going to come to me, and try to turn me back from this call, and that He would come to me by way of my loved ones (See Matthew 10:36). I had a real battle with the enemy when I was first called to the ministry. It would sometimes take me three hours to go to sleep. At that time I did not pray in the Spirit, and I had to call on Jesus out of my limited reasoning, and I went to sleep calling on Jesus. There were all kinds of things trying to hinder that call and most of it came through my loved ones.

And you will find that many times loved ones will remind you of your past. It was rough for a SEASON concerning me. They used to say, "Here comes holy Joe. I knew you when you were doing this or that." It becomes important to know you are called. You've got to know that you know that you know that you're called. That call will keep you. You can live on that call because that is what your whole life is about. The call becomes the motivation of your life (See Acts 20:24). It really is! Your secular job is secondary. Anything else you do is secondary. It is all to this end, to get you to the place where God can fully bring you into the ministry He has for you (See Romans 8:28). So your loved ones will be affected by God's call and commission to you.

"And therefore I have sworn unto the house of Eli, that the iniquity of Eli's house shall not be purged with sacrifice nor offering forever. There is a point beyond grace after repeated admonition (See Proverbs 29:1). And Samuel lay until the morning, and opened the doors of the house of the LORD. And Samuel feared to shew Eli the vision. Then Eli called Samuel, and said, Samuel, my son. And he answered, Here am I. And he said, What **is** the thing that the **LORD** hath said unto thee? I pray thee hide it not from me: God do so to thee, and more also, if thou hide **anything** from me of all the things that he said unto thee. And Samuel told him every whit, and hid nothing from him. And he said, It **is** the LORD: let him do what seemeth him good. And Samuel grew, and the LORD was with him, and did let none of his words fall to the ground. And all Israel from Dan even to Beersheba knew that Samuel **was** established **to be** a prophet of the LORD. And the LORD appeared again in Shiloh by the word of the LORD" (1 Samuel 3:14-21).

Shiloh, derived from the Hebrew word 'shalah,' means a place of security, a place of safety, a place of assurance. Summarized, it means a place of rest! When you are not at rest in the call of God, He cannot say very much to you because you will go overboard or underboard. You must come to a spiritual Shiloh, a place of safety and security where you are not wavering to and fro, in and out of the world, in and out of oppression, in and out of these things. God cannot use you because you take His things and you misuse them. He is waiting for you to come to a place of stability. Some folks say, "I've got to be used; I've got to do this or I've got to do that." That in itself shows that you have not come to Shiloh yet. By your fidgeting and saying, "I just have to, I must." That is not the place of Shiloh. "The wisdom that is from above is first pure, then peaceable" . . . (James 3:17).

One of the hardest things I had to do was say, "Lord, I take this ministry and I give it right back to you," because when it is all said and done, He is going to do it anyway. I had my own concept of ministry that was contrary to what God had called me to. I had purposed to minister and be used a certain way, and God had something entirely different. I had to submit the ministry to Him. After all, its really His ministry in me.

You must come to a place of not maneuvering and trying to make ministry come forth. If it's God, it is going to come forth (See Philippians 2:13). If it's you, it is not going to come forth; that is not **real** ministry of God. When you get out of the way your ministry will come forth (See John 15:4-5). It has to come forth; nobody can stop it. But if you are in the way, you are going nowhere. Once I said to the Lord, "I don't care if I'm ever used just as long as I am in Your will." The word comes and God begins to reveal His purpose when you come to the place of security, safety and assurance; when you come to **Shiloh**.

The word can only be released to do its full work in us when we come to a place of rest in the Lord. "Receive with meekness the **engrafted** word, which is able to save your souls" (James 1:21). The Greek word for **engrafted** is translated `emphutos,' which means **implanted**, or the word that has come to a position of rest within. It is only that type of word that will save (*deliver, protect, heal, preserve, make whole*) your soul. Then the Lord will truly be revealed in us. Paul said that God separated and called me, "...to reveal His Son in me, that I might preach..." (Galatians 1:16).

THE CALLING OF THE APOSTLES

As we look at the calling of the Apostles, it is necessary to emphasize that there has to be a divine encounter with God for a call. "And it came to pass in those days, that He (talking about Jesus) went out into a mountain to pray, and continued all night in prayer to God. And when it was day, He called

unto him His disciples: and of them He **chose** twelve, whom also He named apostles" (Luke 6:12-13). There were more than twelve to come unto Him, but he chose twelve. He went through very careful prayer. Even though He was God manifested in the flesh, He was in prayer all night. It is a serious thing to be called of God. Jesus counted it very serious, enough to communicate with His Father all night concerning the calling of the apostles. We continually see that a divine encounter was involved in a call.

> **"Again the next day after John stood, and two of his disciples; And looking upon Jesus as He walked, he saith, Behold the Lamb of God! And the two disciples heard Him speak and they followed Jesus"   (John 1:35-37).**

Here they had a divine encounter with Jesus. All they did was hear Jesus **speak**, and they followed Him.

> **"Then Jesus turned, and saw them following, and saith unto them, What seek ye? They said unto him, Rabbi, *(being interpreted, 'Master')*. Where dwellest thou? He saith unto them, Come and see. They came and saw where he dwelt, and abode with him that day: for it was about the tenth hour *(about 4 o'clock)*. One of the two which heard John speak, and followed him, was Andrew and Simon Peter's brother. He first findeth his own brother Simon, and saith unto him, We have found the Messiah, which is, being interpreted the Christ. And he brought him to Jesus. And when Jesus beheld him, He said, Thou art Simon the son of Jona: thou shalt be called Cephas, which is by interpretation, a stone.**

> **The day following Jesus would go forth into Galilee, and findeth Philip, and saith unto him, Follow me. Now Philip was of Bethsaida, the city of Andrew and Peter. Philip findeth Nathanael, and saith unto him, We have found**

him, of whom Moses in the law, and the prophets, did write, Jesus of Nazareth, the son of Joseph. And Nathanael said unto him, Can there any good thing come out of Nazareth? Philip saith unto him, Come and see. Jesus saw Nathanael coming to him, and saith of him, Behold an Israelite indeed, in whom is no guile! Nathanael saith unto him, Whence knowest thou me? *(Remember He told Jeremiah: I have known thee since your mother's womb and ordained you.)* Jesus answered and said unto him, Before that Philip called thee, when thou wast under the fig tree, I saw thee. *(I want you to know that whoever God has called, His eye is upon them and He watches their lives, even before they know He is watching them)* Nathanael answered and saith unto him, Rabbi, thou art the Son of God; thou art the King of Israel. *(See, Nathanael confessed that He was the Son of God, even as Peter did)* Jesus answered and said unto him, Because I said unto thee, I saw thee under the fig tree, believest thou? Thou shalt see greater things than these. And he saith unto him, Verily, verily, I say unto you, Hereafter ye shall see heaven open, and the angels of God ascending and descending upon the Son of man
(John 1:38-51).

Each one of these men were involved in a divine encounter with Jesus, which resulted in a change of mind, a change of direction and a change of attitude, because they were **touched** by His presence, even before He said very much. And Jesus even commissioned them, and told them to do something. He said, "Follow Me." That was all they were asked to do right then, but they accepted and obeyed His command. Many people never say yes to the Lord's command to "Follow Me." Let us, with all our hearts, put aside all excuses and say "YES LORD," and FOLLOW HIM!

CHAPTER 5

MANY ARE CALLED,
BUT FEW ARE CHOSEN

I pray that some of the things that the Lord has made real in me can be imparted to you. It will save you a lot of headaches if you can keep from having to learn these things the hard way. It will eliminate some of your confusion and lack of direction.

"And Jesus answered and spake unto them again by parables, and said, The kingdom of heaven is like unto a certain king, which made a marriage for his son, And sent forth his servants to call them that were bidden to the wedding: and they would not come" (Matthew 22:1-3).

See, the initial call is very minute as far as bringing us into the ministry. The call is the first thing, like walking in the door. It is like walking in a church building for a service. The service has not started; you have just walked in the door. That is a similar comparison.

In this particular parable, God did call many, but many of them did not even accept the call. In verse 3, we read: "And sent forth his servants to call them that were bidden to the wedding: and they would not come. ....Behold, I have prepared my dinner: my oxen and my fatlings are killed, and all things are ready: come unto the marriage" (Verse 4). Come in union with Me and get in step with Me. Become one with Me. Become one in my purpose. Become one in My service. Become one in My work. "But they made light of it..." (Verse 5). Some people make light of their call. By the way they act toward their call, it brings reproach to the Lord. I would rather that they wouldn't say that they were called, if their lives don't reflect the character of a minister. Be careful when you use the title "Reverend, or Pastor, etc."

I'm going to admit something. God has had to help me to keep the right attitude, because I don't understand why God has called some people. I don't understand it, but I'm glad it is not left up to me. I do know He calls sinners, because I was one.

When you are called to a place, especially when you are publicly known as a minister, remember that the minister is a reflection of that place. When you say that you are a minister and ordained in a particular church, if you are not walking right with God, shut your mouth. You cause a bad reputation to be upon the church, which may not be deserved. Many people who say they are called to preach bring reproach to Jesus because of the type of lives they live, the type of things that they do, and the places where they are seen.

As a pastor, you can get upset about a lot of things if you want to. I am learning that people are the Lord's sheep anyway, and if the Lord has planted them in the church, I will love them no matter what they do, although I may find it necessary to correct them. It may shake me for a moment, but God has given me a vision of the people and their calling and if they do something that is really out of the way, I'll cool down because God will put the vision of His purpose for them before me. Do you know you have to have a vision to minister to people? (See

Proverbs 29:18) You have to have a vision of them in order to help them or people will frustrate you. You will get tired but, thank God, He gives you a vision, and when you might react in yourself, God says, "But look, I said this." "Oh, yes Lord, that is what they are going to be." Then you can back off even though you are mad. I've wanted to be mad with certain people, but I couldn't. The Lord said, "I don't want you to be mad at them. I'm dealing with them and they are too sensitive right now. I'll teach them another way." Sometimes, it is the reverse and He says, "You let them know I don't like this and I mean I don't like it."

If God has called you and you stay faithful to that call, eventually you will be more in tune with the emotion of God. Sometimes, I go home and listen to the tapes of a message I've preached and I say, "My goodness, why am I so mad?" Then the Lord said, "You are mad, because I am mad." Whew! It gets to me, because as a pastor I have on the job training, too.

But the Lord went out and called them and they made light of it. Don't make light of a call. It is a privilege to be called of God. In fact, it's the highest calling on Earth! "But they made light of it, and went their ways..." (Verse 5). Oh, Jesus, deliver us from our ways. That's half the battle right there. "...They went their own ways, one to his farm, another to his merchandise: And the remnant took his servants, and entreated them spitefully, and slew them. But when the king heard thereof, he was wroth: and he sent forth his armies, and destroyed those murderers, and burned up their city. Then saith he to his servants, the wedding is ready, but they which were bidden were not worthy" (Verses 5-8).

Now, they were worthy in Christ, yet they did not accept the bid, then He said they were not worthy. "Go ye therefore into the highways, and as many as ye shall find, bid to the marriage. So those servants went out into the highways, and gathered together all as many as they found, both bad and good: and the wedding was furnished with guests" (Verses 9-10). In this parable, we can see why not many noble, not many wise are called; because they trust in their own wisdom and have what they call logical excuses which hinder them from choosing and accepting the call of God. They don't choose to give into God's election (See 1 Corinthians 1:26-29; 2 Peter 1:10). "For many are called, but few **are** chosen" (Verse 14).

The way to be **chosen** is to **accept** the call God gives. God called these men and they did not choose to accept the call; they were not chosen. 'I know I am called to preach, but I have to do this and I have to do that.' They really did not **accept** the call. They accepted it on their own terms and through their ideologies. You can't come unto God by your own terms, but it is by His terms! 'Well, I'll preach if...' They did not really **accept** the call. We want to be **chosen** of God, not just called, but **chosen**! Chosen for what? Chosen, so that God can give you all that you are supposed to have with your call.

You can begin to move into the call He has given you with everything He's got for you. To be **chosen**, God can grant to you and put at your disposal, whatever enablement you need to accomplish what He has called you to do. That cannot be by your accepting only part of His way, mixed with your ways. It has to be HIM all the way. The question is, do you really want to be **chosen**? Thank God, you are called, but do you want to be **chosen**? I want to be **chosen** that God may say, "Here, you have accepted the call and you've yielded to the call and you've let the call deal with you. Now, I **choose** you! Because many are called, but few are **chosen** and that is why, when the call comes, people don't line their lives up with the call. They get the call and go on about their own business doing their own thing. They are not ready to be the **chosen**. They don't want to be the **chosen of God** for a particular thing, or a particular commission. When you are **chosen**, it is because God has called you, and you have lined your life up with that call. You've allowed the Lord to work in you and through you whatever He has to do to get you to the place that you are a vessel, not of wood and stubble, but of gold.

"I called him, and he gave in to that call, and his life-style changed according to that call, and his family gave in to that call. His finances, his physical life, everything gave in to that call. Now, I choose him to go." There is something more than the call. We discussed the call and it was important, but how about being **chosen**? You are being made to be chosen! And there must be a cleansing.

You know you are called; that is settled. Many are called. We want you to recognize when you are called. But that is not the end of it, because a lot of people are called, but not too many are **chosen**. Let's continue in this progression.

RECOGNIZING OUR SPIRITUAL CONDITION WHEN CALLED

Let's look again at Isaiah, Chapter 6, which is an account of Isaiah's call. After Isaiah had seen the LORD, he had to see his own state. Isaiah said, "Then said I, Woe is me." (Verse 5) What a terrible wretched state I am in, for I am undone.

Isaiah said, "Woe is me, for I am undone." He admitted it. God could deal with him then. A lot of us think that we can do it, but we can't. "Lord, I'm undone. I'm not full. I'm not consecrated yet." What does the word "consecrated" mean? To be full of, an open hand, filled. It is the act of setting apart anything or person to the worship or service of God. It is to be an indication of power or a means, or direction. "For I dwell in the midst of a people with unclean lips," Isaiah said, "for mine eyes have seen the King, the LORD of hosts." He admitted his state and God did something about it. "Then the LORD laid a live coal upon his mouth" (Verse 7). He began to purge Isaiah. He took a coal off the altar and He brought it and laid it upon Isaiah's mouth and said, "Lo, this hath touched thy mouth." The altar was a type of the heart; therefore, God began to deal with Isaiah's heart. Most of the time the Lord listens to our heart anyway, because that's where He can get in. Your heart will say, `Lord, I know that I'm not the way that I should be.' Your mind will say, `Oh, you're all right.' But in your heart where Christ dwells, you will say, `I'm wrong. I'm undone.' Then the Lord can deal with that, for all His works are done in truth (See Psalms 33:4). What is the result? He laid a live coal upon his mouth. He began action, and said, "Lo, this hath touched thy lips; and thine iniquity is taken away, and thy sin purged." Then Isaiah could go speak to the people. In scripture, we are admonished to, ". . . Be ye clean that bear the things of the Lord..." (Isaiah 52:11b).

We must recognize that we are called, we must have a divine encounter with God, and we must be consecrated and separated. We are to be made vessels that can hold the anointing *(the Holy Spirits divine enablement)*. We must minister under the anointing given according to our calling. The anointing must be entrusted to you, where every area of your life and ministry reflects the Anointed One.

THE ANOINTING IS TO CAUSE YOU TO BE

As stated previously, the anointing is there when you are called, but that anointing comes basically to consecrate and cleanse you.

The anointing is to cause you **to be**, so that you are such a vessel consecrated to Him that when you move your hand, you're preaching the Word of God. When you stare at somebody, you are preaching to them. You are such an open hand, that God can even speak and preach to others by who you are, and not just by what you say and do. For many people, Jesus just looked at them and they followed Him. That's **real** ministry.

The Word must become flesh. Everything Jesus did was the Word of God. We have recorded what Jesus did. Some of that which is written is just a narrative of what He did. But what is that narrative to us? It's the Word of God. If he reached out, that was the Word of God. He wants everything that you do to be an expression of Himself. If you step out on the platform, you purport the will of God. If you don't say anything, but just look, you are saying and displaying the Word of God. In everything that you do, make sure it is an expression of the Word of God. That's **real** ministry! "And the Word was made flesh and dwelt among us, and we beheld His glory..." (John 1:14).

The ministry cannot be something outside of you. You can't separate the ministry from the person. You just can't do it. That's why the Lord wants everything about you to be ministry. Just to look at people, you are preaching to them. Especially in the priestly ministry of praise and worship, He wants your whole life lined up with the anointing to worship, so He can trust you with it all. He's working on everything about you, to line up with the call He has given you. Sometimes we jump the gun, but God must first allow the anointing to change you so He can give you the anointing to manifest Himself (See John 1:12, Ephesians 1:12; 3:7; II Corinthians 3:5-7; John 12:24).

SEPARATION UNTO MINISTRY

There is an anointing which comes with the call, though the anointing may not manifest itself in an outward display. It manifests itself in your inner-life. The anointing first comes to consecrate **you**. The anointing comes at first to cause you to come into the realm of consecration or cleansing, and it comes to separate you. Later on, the anointing for fulfillment of what the Lord said comes. Some people get mixed up and say, 'I've got the anointing.' But what is the anointing for right **now**? The anointing right now is to consecrate **you**. The anointing is to clean **you** up and to separate **you**. This is where people really miss it. This is the period where there is going to be some craving of flesh, of your ways, and of doing your thing (See 2 Timothy 2:21,22). When I mention **anointing**, I'm speaking in simple terms of God's Divine enablement and ability through the Holy Spirit. Broken down, it is a union of the Word and Spirit released in you, or Christ, the Anointed One, coming forth in all His nature, character and power.

When you are called, God grants an anointing to cleanse you and to get you **ready** to fulfill that call. Once He grants the anointing, He is waiting on everything in your life to come in line with the anointing in that call. That call must affect every area of your life. As a result of that call, God is waiting for you to put off everything contrary to His nature. Whatever I plan should be as a result of the fact that I'm called, and that I have had an encounter with God. When God has spoken and told you something that He wants done, He is waiting on that life to line up with that call. But that first realm of the anointing comes to deal with **you** and to consecrate **you**.

Sometimes when we are called we are ready to run, but, wait a minute, you are undone. Remember, He called a sinner, and one that's unfit. He called you out of nowhere. Now let Him deal with your life. The anointing has come to enable you to move into the right style of life, so that after you have given in to the call, and the anointing that comes initially with the call, the Lord can grant you the anointing to **fulfill** what He has called you to do. That anointing increases, because He will give you a greater release of the anointing (*or more Divine enablement*) as you progress in your call. Another call, another commission, and again the anointing comes for the fulfillment of it.

Many of you are called to the ministry, called to preach, and do you know what is happening? God is preparing you **for the anointing** - by the anointing. The anointing is there, but the anointing has come to get **you** together, to change your ways and your ideas, lift you up to God's ways and to get your life separated and consecrated unto Him (See Ephesians 3:7). So, by the anointing **to be**, you are prepared for the anointing **to do**. It sounds like double talk, but it's true. You are being prepared by the anointing for the anointing and you can run and try **to do** at this level of the anointing **to be** and it doesn't have any effects. Without the anointing, there is no manifestation of Christ. It is the anointing that destroys the yoke of bondage in the people of God (See Isaiah 10:27b).

So the call is sure. Now, what is happening? God is granting the anointing to consecrate **you**, to separate **you**, and to change

you. The most important thing that we must do as ministers is give in to this process of the anointing.

When you recognize the call, and you have had a Divine encounter, then eventually the Church recognizes that the call of God is on your life and that God has commissioned you. Though it may be a general commission, God grants to you an anointing, but that anointing is not **to do** yet. That anointing is **to be**! That is the anointing that comes with the call. **It is to be!** He wants us **to be** by the anointing, according to what we have been given. The Lord wants our lives to change and everything about us to begin to change because of that anointing.

Prayer is not something you **do**; it is the thing you are! You are a prayer! We make prayer a ritual and it is not a ritual. Prayer is not something you **do**; prayer is something you are! I am a pray-er; I'm praying all the time, praying about everything. 'Lord, what shall I say?' You reach a place where you are in constant prayer. Your first reaction to anything is to pray! That is when you are labeled a pray-er (See 1 Thessalonians 5:7, Psalms 109:4). When you become a worshipper, you always worship. It is a part of your being. In the same way, when we are talkers, we always talk. It is part of our being. Some of us are a little bit more talkative than others.

Because of this Divine Encounter and this call, there must be a separation, a consecration, and a cleansing, to prepare for the anointing **to do**. The anointing that came with the call which we just discussed, is **to be**! Now we are getting ready for the anointing **to do**!

CHAPTER 6

THE CALL OF PAUL
THE NEW TESTAMENT PROCESS

Let's look at Acts 9, and the call of Apostle Paul. I feel close to Paul, almost like I know him. I seem close to Paul because what he has done is eternal. The implications and power of the Word that Paul left us is still working today in our lives, and I can say personally in my life.

The word 'Saul' means 'destroyer.' The name 'Paul' means 'worker.' He was turned from a destroyer to a worker. A real call of God is going to change your nature! "And Saul, yet breathing out threatenings and slaughter against the disciples of the Lord, went unto the high priest, And desired of him letters to Damascus to the synagogues, that if he found any of this way, whether they were men or women, he might bring them bound unto Jerusalem" (Acts 9:1,2).

Now, under the order we just showed you in Samuel, Jeremiah and Isaiah the church didn't exist then, so it was all based upon God. He had to teach them, commission them, and guide them through the whole process, and He is still involved in the process today! In the New Testament dispensation, we see things a little different. "And as he journeyed, he came near Damascus: and suddenly there shined round about him a light from heaven" (Verse 3). There was a Divine Encounter that changed his life! "And he fell to the Earth..." (Verse 4)

Whenever you have a Divine Encounter, flesh is going to have to get out of the way. You have to see change in those people's lives. If you are called to the ministry, you can't keep doing the same things you have done. You just can't. You're a spectacle. People look at you on purpose, and God wants them to look at you! "...And heard a voice saying unto him..." (Verse 4). Again, he **heard** a voice. He didn't think he heard a voice, but he **knew** he heard a voice. "...Saul, Saul, why persecutest thou me?" (Verse 4). "And he said, Who art thou, Lord? And the Lord said, I am Jesus whom thou persecutest: it is hard for thee to kick against the pricks" *(which means, it is hard for thee to go against My purpose and My plan)* (Verse 5) "and he trembling and astonished said, Lord, what wilt thou have me to do?..." (Verse 6). He knew there was something for him to do. How did he know? God must have spoken to him, or he must have had a knowing inside, because He answered and responded to him knowing that there was something for him to do. "...And the Lord **said** unto him, Arise, and go into the city, and it shall be told thee what thou must do" (Verse 6).

Under our dispensation in the New Testament, God has placed His authority in and through Christ Jesus and Jesus has placed His authority in the **Church**. Though Paul had a Divine Encounter with the Lord, the church is the instrument where the Lord manifests His power and His authority. Though he had a Divine Encounter with the Lord, He turned him back over to the church. Your call is depending upon you and God, yet He will not bypass His Body. He will turn you over to the church, and the authority to move forth in what the Lord has called you to, will come through the Church. He does not bypass His church (See Ephesians 1:22-23; 3:20-21).

Though you have a Divine Encounter, and the Lord person-ally calls you aside and tells you something that He wants you to do, the authority to do it will come through the Church. He turns you over to the Church. He will not bypass His order, and His order is through His church. His desire and purpose flows through His Church. He is not going to go and talk to somebody, and not talk to His own Body. He turned Paul over to the Church and said, "**Go** and it shall be told you."

We are going to find that before he started moving forth into his call, it was almost fourteen years. Paul had a lot of unlearn-ing to do. If he had gone out and preached the way he was, with a destroyer nature, he would have taken the things of God and wreaked havoc. He was turned over to the church and the Lord sent a disciple named Ananias and gave Paul his commis-sion.

Now, why did He do that? Because part of the purpose of the Church is that He join together in **one** body, many tongues and kindreds, out of many nations. He is bringing to pass, as a part of His witness this prayer of Jesus in John 17:21, "That they might be **one** as Thou, Father, art in Me, and I in Thee."

THE NEW TESTAMENT PROCESS OF MINISTRY - IN AND THROUGH THE BODY

"I therefore, the prisoner of the Lord, beseech you that ye walk worthy of the vocation *(or ministry)* wherewith ye are called, *(in verse 2 he tells you how)* With all lowliness and meek-ness, with long suffering, forbearing one another in love" (Eph-esians 4:1-2). `Wait a minute, you say, what does my vocation and my calling have to do with someone else?' Everything-because in the Body of Christ, they all fit together and there can be no ministry outside of the body. All ministry of the Lord is done in the Body and **through** the Body (See Ephesians 4:16).

A lot of folks have ruined their ministry potential, because they feel like they have been called, yet they have never fully given themselves to a fellowship. They have never come under authority or submitted to a Church body, and they run out and do much damage. We are first to minister one to another (See I Peter 4:10). They have no feelings nor love for the people. They make mincemeat of the people and ruin people's lives. They don't know the frailty of themselves yet. They have taken the call of God and ran with it, knowing nothing about God's ways. I've known people that say, "I don't need to go to any local assembly!" I know that they are in error, because it is not God's divine order and it is not God's way. That is contrary to Scripture, and if you do not have something to balance you, then you have your own law (See Romans 10:1-3). They say, `God told me to; I don't care what the Scriptures say.' But what is the balancing factor? You have no safety! God always speaks in the balance of the Scriptures. I have heard people say, "The Lord said this...Listen, God speaks to me and that is the only person I can hear from. I never hear it confirmed. I never hear it a second time."

My answer to them is, "That is why you are in the trouble you are in right now. The effects show that you don't hear anybody." "...In the mouth of two or three witnesses shall every **word** be established" (2 Corinthians 13:1b), **word** meaning `rhema,' which is the word made spirit and life and the word made a voice. It has to be spoken before it becomes life and is established, "out of the mouth of two or three witnesses."

Now, your call with God and your encounter with Him is based on your relationship with Him, but He is going to confirm it and the ministry is going to prove itself in the Church. It is going to flow forth and everybody is going to recognize the call that is upon your life (See Galatians 2:9). It will come forth in God's timetable. It is based upon you, but it is also based on Him. He has a timetable and He knows what He is doing. He knows about eternal things; we don't know about eternity. The thing you need to do is recognize the call, accept the call, and take heed to the commission and to follow the call.

The Lord turned Paul over to the Church. Though I am in active ministry, I am in the school of Christ, I am still being made, and I've got a lot more areas in which to be made, but I can honestly say that the Church has oiled me up. I use that term 'oil me up,' and you are going to understand it in subsequent chapters when I begin to deal with the subject of, "the anointing that abides." You're going to understand that it is not just a slang term, but it is something that is real and meaningful to a minister to say, 'I've been oiled up.'

You must realize the meaning of 'impartation.' Where I am in the Lord has a lot to do with the established and proven ministries that I was around during my time of training. God meant it that way because what they have is in the Holy Spirit; it is not theirs. "...A man can receive nothing, except it be given him from heaven..." (John 3:27).

I remember one time telling Pastor A.J. Rowden of the Evangelistic Center Church something *(there was a little difficulty between us at the time)* and I did not speak to him in the right spirit. I had to go back and apologize to him, asking forgiveness of God later on. The Lord was in what I was talking about, but I did not do it in the right attitude. I said, 'Listen, I did not come down here to receive your personality; I came in here to receive the deposit of God that He has given you and that's what I want.' He was a wise man and said, 'Yes, and you're going to get every bit of it if it kills you.' And, you know, it did, because I had a hard time submitting to a church that was completely different from my background.

That was where much of my humbling process came in training, by just submitting to Brother Rowden. God turned me over to that Church and there was not much that I did while I was there. Oh, I was used in the ministry; I worked with Teen Challenge and with some street ministries. I taught Bible school and Bible classes in a denominational church, but I was not really productive until the authority came through the Church where the Lord sent me. There was not much that was productive because the source on earth is the Body. That is the instrument He uses.

Pastor Rowden knew when it was time that I was to be sent out. A lot of other folks did not understand the process God had ordained for me, and they came against him. 'Who is Jeff Edwards? Where did he come from? We don't know him; where did he come from?' But Brother and Sister Rowden heard from God, concerning my time of ordination and commission to move forth in the vision the Lord had given me.

When God sets you in a place and it is time for you to go, they must let you go at your appointed time. If they don't, their ministry will be hindered, because it becomes a part of their ministry to nourish you, to confirm you, to build you up to the place that God can send you forth. This is a part of their ministry, and if they don't let you go when it is your time to go, then they are not fulfilled in their ministry, and the anointing will in a sense be lifted because they are not obeying God.

I want you to know that there are a lot of things that try to shake the training process of the Lord. I encountered race problems. I encountered problems where some people just did not like young people. I encountered a lot of things. But that is what made me. How I reacted to those things was the test in my training. I had plenty of opportunity to have a bad attitude, especially concerning the race matter, because I was a strong racist in the past. Many times, I had real opportunity to use that racism as leverage, but I knew what my flesh was trying to do. It was trying to make me ruin the ministry that God had given me. And my heart said, "No, that is not the way. Except I come through the door the right way, I am thief and I am a robber."

In Acts 9:7-17 we read:

"And the men which journeyed with him stood speechless, hearing a voice, but seeing no man. And Saul arose from the earth; and when his eyes were opened, he saw no man: but they led him by the hand, and brought him into Damascus. And he was three days without sight, and neither did eat nor drink. And there was a certain disciple at Damascus, named Ananias; and to him said the Lord in a vision, Ananias. And he said, Behold, I am here, Lord. And the Lord said unto him, Arise, and go into the street which is called Straight, and enquire in the house of Judas for one called Saul, of Tarsus; for, behold, he prayeth, And hath seen in a vision a man named Ananias coming in, and putting his hand on him, that he might receive his sight. *(Jesus endorses the laying on of hands right here).* Then Ananias answered, Lord, I have heard by many of this man, how much evil he hath done to thy saints at Jerusalem: And here he hath authority from the chief priests to bind all that call on thy name. But the Lord said unto him, Go thy way: for he is a chosen vessel unto me, to bear my name before the Gentiles,

and kings, and the children of Israel: For I will shew him
how great things he must suffer for my name's sake. And
Ananias went his way, and entered into the house; and
putting his hands on him said, Brother Saul, the Lord, even
Jesus, that appeared unto thee in the way as thou
camest, hath sent me, that thou mightest receive thy
sight, and be filled with the Holy Ghost" (Acts 9:7-17).

And Paul said in his own testimony in Acts 22nd chapter
that it was Ananias that gave him the commission. God gave
him the call initially, but there is a difference in the New
Testament process. He gives you the knowing, but the commission or the authority for the commission comes through the
Church. There has to be this balancing factor.

Paul, talking to the Jews, "And I said, What shall I do, Lord?
And the Lord said unto me, Arise, and go into Damascus; and
there it shall be **told** thee of all things which are **appointed for
thee to do**" (Acts 22:10). God is saying, Go on back to the
Church. Since I have called you, the Church is going to know
about it. You just accept the call; that is your responsibility.

"And when I could not see for the glory of that light, being
led by the hand of them that were with me, I came into
Damascus.
And one Ananias, a devout man according to the law,
having a good report of all the Jews which dwelt there,
Came unto me, and stood, and said unto me, Brother
Saul, receive thy sight. And the same hour I looked up
upon him. And he said, *(he began to prophesy to him)*
the God of our fathers hath chosen thee, that thou
shouldest know his will, and see that Just One, and
shouldest hear the voice of His mouth. For thou shalt be
His witness unto all men of what thou hast seen and
heard. And now why tarriest thou? Arise, and be bap-

tized, and wash away thy sins, calling on the name of the Lord" (Acts 22:11-16). So, the commission of Paul was given through the Church.

When you know you are called of God and God touches your life, and there is a divine encounter with God, then the next process is the hardest. This is the period that comes after the Divine Encounter which is **separation, consecration** and **cleansing** to prepare for the anointing (See Romans 1:1).

PAUL - A CONTAINER FOR THE ANOINTING

Let's look further at the life of Paul. Paul was called in Acts, Chapter 9, and was not used on a continual basis until Chapter 11, when Barnabas went to get him to come down to Antioch, because the church was growing so rapidly. Here he was used in the local church ministry, probably as an assistant pastor. He came to Antioch three or four years after he was called. After about ten years, he was sent out in Acts 13:1-4 as an assistant or associate missionary. This was approximately thirteen or fourteen years after his initial call to preach. He was called and anointed initially, but he was being **made** as a vessel to hold the anointing. Paul was to carry a very difficult message and he was to be involved in a ministry that would bring much suffering. He had to be **made**, and had to learn to abide in the anointing of God.

In Ephesians 3:1, we see that Paul knew his calling. "For this cause I Paul, the prisoner of Jesus Christ for you Gentiles. *(I'm in bondage to this call. I'm in bondage to Jesus).* If ye have heard of the dispensation of the grace of God which is given me to you-ward: How that by revelation he made known unto me the mystery; *(as I wrote afore in few words, Whereby, when ye read, ye may understand my knowledge in the mystery of Christ)"* (Ephesians 3:1-4).

There are some things that go with a commission that God has called you to, that have never been revealed before. He has reserved it for someone special whom He has called, to bring that revelation forth to the Church. It may be revealed in a measure in the word, but not in the measure of understanding God wants for this dispensation.

> **"Which in other ages was not made known unto the sons of men, as it is now revealed unto his holy apostles and prophets by the Spirit; That the Gentiles should be fellow heirs, and of the same body, and partakers of his promise in Christ by the gospel: Whereof I was made a minister..." (Ephesians 3:5-7).**

To what was I **made** a minister? According to what He called me to. You wear God's clothing according to what God has called you to. "...According to the gift of the grace of God given unto me by the **effectual** working of His power *(effectual means operative or active working of His power)*" (Ephesians 3:7). Paul said, "I was **made** to do what I was called to do. You made me. You dealt with me throughout my whole life." God was making Paul for the anointing to come upon his life and to **abide**.

Colossians, Chapter 1, is acknowledging Christ's preeminence and recognizing that all fullness is in **HIM**, but this same principle of being made is seen. "Whereof I am **made a minister** *(He's done what? Made a minister.)*, according to this dispensation of God which is given to me for you, to fulfill the Word of God" (Colossians 1:25). A dispensation *(plan or arrangement of purpose)* was given to me to fulfill the Word of God. Consecration means to be full of, filled, or fully able. This grace was given to Paul to fulfill the Word of God out of acknowledging His preeminence.

"Forasmuch then as Christ hath suffered for us in the flesh, arm yourselves likewise with the same mind:..." (I Peter 4:1). This is part of the artillery you must wear. This is part of your weaponry. Arm yourself with what? The knowledge that Christ suffered for us in the flesh. By your arming yourself with the knowledge of Christ, it becomes a weapon. "...For he that hath suffered in the flesh hath ceased from sin; That he no longer should live the rest of his time in the flesh to the lusts of men, but to the will of God" (I Peter 4:1-2). That is why God is **making** you, to deliver you from the lusts of men or the lust of your own flesh, that you can be **made** to conform to the will of God.

> **"For the time past of our life may suffice us to have wrought the will of the Gentiles, when we walked in lasciviousness, lusts, excess of wine, revellings, banquetings, and abominable idolatries; Wherein they think it strange that ye run not with them to the same excess of riot, speaking evil of you** *(you stopped running with the people who do all those things and they think you are strange, but the Lord told you to get out of all that stuff)*: **Who shall give account to him that is ready to judge the quick and the dead. For this cause was the gospel preached also to them that are dead, that they might be judged according to men in the flesh, but live according to God in the Spirit. But the end of all things is at hand: be ye therefore sober, and watch unto prayer. And above all things have fervent** *(white-heated)* **charity among yourselves: for charity shall cover the multitude of sins. Use hospitality one to another without grudging. As every man hath received the gift, even so minister the**

same one to another, as good stewards *(or trustees)* **of the manifold grace of God. If any man speak, let him speak as the oracles of God; if any man minister, let him do it as of the ability which God giveth: that God in all things may be glorified through Jesus Christ, to whom be praise and dominion forever and ever. Amen"**

(I Peter 4:3-11)

Who gives the ability? God gives the ability. He's **making** you, that He might give you the enablement you need **to do!** We minister according to what God gives, but a lot is up to us. We must be in the place where God can give, so **we can be,** and **we can do!** We minister according to the **ability that God gives!** It is based on **HIM!** God giveth! And this is so that God can be glorified through Jesus Christ.

"But we have this treasure in earthen vessels, that the excellency of the power my be of God, and not of us" (2 Corinthians 4:7). It is HIS power. It is not us. What He wants us to do is conform ourselves to that anointing that is given **to do.** He wants us to give in to the anointing He has given us **to do,** so that the excellency of the power may be of God, and not of ourselves.

"Not that we are sufficient of ourselves to think anything as of ourselves; but our sufficiency is of God; Who also hath *made* **us able ministers of the new testament..."**

(2 Corinthians 3:5-6)

CHAPTER 7

THE PROCESS OF MINISTRY
IN THE CALL OF ELISHA

Look at I Kings 19:12 when Elisha was called. Elijah had fled to the mountains looking for God:

"And after the earthquake a fire; but the LORD was not in the fire: and after the fire a still small voice. And it was so, when Elijah heard it, that he wrapped his face in his mantle, and went out, and stood in the entering of the cave. And, behold, there came a voice unto him, and said, What doest thou here, Elijah? And he said, I have been very jealous for the LORD God of hosts: because the children of Israel have forsaken thy covenant, thrown down thine altars, and slain thy prophets with the sword; and I, even I only, am left; and they seek my life, to take it away. And the LORD said unto him, Go return on thy way to the wilderness of Damascus: and when thou comest, anoint Hazael to be king over Syria: And Jehu the son of Nimshi shalt then anoint to be King over Israel: and Elisha the son of Shaphat of Abelmeholah shalt thou anoint to be prophet in thy room. And it shall come to pass, that him that escapeth the sword of Hazael shall Jehu slay: and him that escapeth from the sword of Jehu shall Elisha slay. Yet I have left me seven thousand in Israel, all the knees which have not bowed unto Baal, and every mouth which hath not kissed him. So he de-

parted thence and found Elisha, the son of Shaphat, who was plowing with twelve yoke of oxen before him, and he the twelve and Elijah passed by him, and cast his mantle upon him. And he left the oxen and ran after Elijah, and said, Let me, I pray thee, kiss my father and my mother and then I will follow thee..." (1 Kings 19:12-20).

It didn't say that Elijah said anything. He just threw his mantle on him. When you get in tune, it's a Divine knowing, you don't have to communicate all the time, you just know. "...And he said unto him, Go back again: for what have I done to thee? And he returned back from him, and took a yoke of oxen, and slew them *(in other words, it was a worship unto God)*, and boiled their flesh with the instruments of the oxen, and gave unto the people, and they did eat. Then he arose, and went after Elijah, and ministered unto him" (Verse 20,21). Elisha burned all his bridges behind him. There was nothing of his old life in which to return to (See Luke 9:62; Phil. 3:13,14).

Right then, the mantle was placed upon him which was a symbol of the anointing during Elijah's day. God used the mantle in Elijah's ministry to anoint Elisha for his ministry. But it was approximately 10 years before Elisha functioned as a prophet fully, even though Elisha's mantle was already placed upon him. After his anointing, he then went into a period of consecration, training, learning, receiving and impartation. Elisha ministered or served Elijah and that qualified him for advancement later on. Now Elisha was in the school of the prophets, but what he was learning in school **practically**, he saw **applicably** in Elijah. Elisha said, "As my soul liveth, I will not leave you." What I'm trying to learn in the books, I see going on right now in action. If I can see and learn the principle of God in action in the life of Elijah, it will be imparted to me.

It was ten years before Elisha was really used. He was going through a period, **to be**, before the anointing came, **to do**. The mantle was placed upon him, **to be**, and it was not a forced thing. In fact, Elijah did everything he could to discourage Elisha. "What have I to do with you?" He just went over and placed his mantle on him, in obedience to God. Then he said, "What do you want? What have I to do with you?"

When there is a call on your life, nothing can push that call back if it's a real call from God (See Romans 8:38-39). Sometimes God does test you and try you, to see where you are coming from, and where your commitment and dedication level is. 'Well, you didn't say it right, and I'm not going to follow,' one might say. If your call is that weak, just because somebody didn't say something to you the way you think it should have been said, you can be assured that your call is questionable. A real call from God could withstand that and a lot more. A **God-call** will stand up to any test.

It was ten years before Elisha came into a full expression of his ministry, though he was anointed when Elijah placed his mantle upon him. But the first anointing is to make you **BE**, before you begin to **DO**. Let us learn God's ways, so you can give in to them and let go of yours, even in your ministry.

THE TESTING OF ELISHA

"And it came to pass, when the Lord would take up Elijah into heaven by a whirlwind, that Elijah went with Elisha from Gilgal. And Elijah said unto Elisha, Tarry here I pray thee: for the Lord hath sent me to Bethel" (2 Kings 2:1).

Some people go through the process of being made for ten years and wind up getting discouraged at the end, and they don't go all the way through the process of God. "He that endured till the end, the same shall be saved" (See Matthew 24:13). Some people start off fast at the beginning. They are excited for a season. But the process of God must continue throughout your experience. After all the things he had gone through, Elisha is again going through another test. Again Elijah is used by God to try to discourage him.

You think God can use somebody to try to discourage you? Sure, He can, and He will. We find out that even though Elisha was under training through Elijah, he knew who called him. Because Elijah, who he was training under, actually discouraged him. But it was the **call of God** that made him stand up. Sometimes God has to make sure that **you** know who you are leaning on. Therefore, He must use even your teacher sometimes to try you, concerning His purpose (See 2 Corinthians 11:23-30). But if there is a real call on your life, you are not going anywhere.

Now if it's based upon a teacher, for example, and if Elisha was just depending upon a teacher when Elijah said unto Elisha, "Get on away from me," he would have cried and gone away with his head tucked down in discouragement, and would have missed his ministry. In fact, he would have never had a ministry, because he was **not** looking unto God as the source. God will, and always has, used human vessels. Elijah was used as a trainer for Elisha, and that was the wisdom of God. I don't really know if Elijah knew what he was doing or not. He just cast his mantle on Elisha and the first thing he said was, "What do I have to do with you?"

As a pastor, some people actually get mad at me because I don't cry when they cry. Sometimes they aren't crying tears caused by a problem or burden, they are just tears of repentance. That doesn't bother me. There are times when some people cry and I just get down with them and cry too. Yet you have to be careful with people, because their tears will fool you. They are not all that you think they are. All your tears and crying don't substitute for obedience to the truth.

He said again, "Tarry here I pray thee, for the Lord hath sent me to Bethel." And Elisha said, `No sir. As the Lord liveth and as thy soul liveth, I will not leave thee.' So they went down to Bethel. Elisha didn't stop. He was down to the final test before coming into effective ministry. Elijah had to make sure that Elisha was ready. He had to make sure that Elisha knew God was his keeper, and that he was depending on God. He was wrapping it up now. It was time for Elisha to come into the realm of the anointing **to do**, and that is when the pressure gets a little intense. God's hand was starting to become heavier. Some of us would break under this final pressure. We might find out we are not ready to go out, so we go through the process again. Have you ever experienced that before? If you ever have, I know you don't want to experience that anymore.

In a similar account, Job was marked toward advancement. You can expect a shedding off of some things when you are marked toward advancement. When you hit rock bottom, you know you are on the way up. This was Elisha's final exam. Have you ever gone through a final exam and clenched up? Through all the teaching you may have gotten good grades, but on the final exam you were clenched up so much that you got a bad grade for the course.

You have to go all the way through the process until that last garment is put upon you; until you are ready to come out and minister in the power of the Spirit, even as Jesus did, after He was tested (See Luke 4:14). I would rather wait and go through the full process, than to come back discouraged, because then you've got to go through a process of ridding yourself of that discouragement. There is a whole new realm of consecration you have to go through to get you out of that defeated state. We get on side roads, and God has to spend time getting us back on the right track, and that takes more time in the preparation process.

Let's continue with Elisha's final testing. "And the sons of the prophets who were at Bethel came forth to Elisha, and said unto him, Knowest thou that the LORD will take away thy master from thy head to day? And he said, Yea, I know it; hold ye your peace" (2 Kings 2:3). They were prophets, therefore, they knew what was going to happen to Elijah, but Elisha said, `Be quiet, I know what's going on.' And Elijah said unto Elisha, "...Tarry here I pray thee, for the LORD hath sent me to Jericho. And he said, As the LORD liveth, and as thy soul liveth, I will not leave thee. So they came to Jericho. And the sons of the prophets of Jericho came to Elisha, and said unto him, Knowest thou that the LORD will take away thy master from thy head to day? And he answered, Yea, I know it; hold ye your peace. And Elijah said unto him, Tarry, I pray thee, here; for the LORD hath sent me to Jordan..." (Verses 4-6).

That last place was to cross over Jordan. That involves spiritual death through denying self. And God will ultimately get to something that we don't want to let go of, even that last cross, crossing the Jordan and dying to self. Let's look at these three places — Bethel, Jericho and Jordan — in relation to Elisha's final testing to qualify him for the anointing, or ability to do, and be sent in a divine commission.

1. Bethel - The Test of the Home and Family - 2 Kings

Bethel is the Hebrew word **'Beyth El'** which means 'house of God.' It comes from another Hebrew root word **'bayith'** which means 'family or home.' The first thing that Elisha had to face in his final test was his **family** and his **home**. He had to determine that he was going to face his home situation. He had to face that place and not stop there, but continue on following the Lord. Many people get stuck at this point. They put their family before their call and their obedience to God. They never leave this 'obstacle,' and that is what the family or home can be if you don't put it in the right place.

In the gospel of Luke, one who wanted to follow Jesus was tested in areas of security of home and he failed. This is the account:

> **"And it came to pass, that, as they went their way a certain man said unto Him, Lord, I will follow thee whithersoever thou goest. And Jesus said unto him, Foxes have holes, and birds of the air have nests; but the Son of Man hath not where to lay his head" (Luke 9:57-58).**

This certain man wanted to follow Jesus, but after he found out that Jesus had no particular place to sleep or lodge, he changed his mind. He was tested in the security of home, and he failed. You never hear of this man anymore.

The next test was in paternal relationship; whether you will follow your natural father or your heavenly Father. "And He said unto another, Follow Me. But he said, Lord, **suffer me first** to go and bury my father" (Luke 9:59). Notice this was the person's first desire, not seeking the Kingdom of God and His righteousness. Many people have things that they want to do **first**, and are not willing to set that aside to answer the call of

God. "Jesus said unto him, let the dead bury their dead: but go thou and preach the kingdom of God" (Verse 60). Again, you never hear of this person anymore. He failed in the area of paternal relationship, in relation to following the Lord and accepting a call to preach.

Then the test in following Jesus was in the area of family relationship. "And another also said, Lord, I will follow thee; but **let me first** go bid them farewell, which are at my **home** at **my house**" (Verse 61). Again, it was a request for "Me first" in the family relationship. This person failed at the principle Jesus gave in another chapter of Luke about being a disciple. "If any man come to Me, and hate not his father, and mother, and wife, and children, and brethren, and sisters, yea, and his own life also, he cannot be My disciple. And whosoever doth not bear his cross, and come after Me, cannot be My disciple" (Luke 14:26-27). The inference here is that your love for, and your desire for His will to be done is so fervent, that anything compared to this love could only be in the category of hate.

Looking back at Luke the 9th chapter, "And Jesus said unto him, No man having put his hand to the plow, and looking back, is fit for the kingdom of God" (Verse 62). Again the inference is directed toward Matthew 6:33, "But seek ye first the kingdom of God and His righteousness; and all these things shall be added unto you."

You never hear of this last person again. He failed in the area of family relationship. In Luke 14:15-24, in the parable of the great supper, many were bidden to come to supper with the Lord, but they had different excuses why they couldn't come. In verse 20, one reply was: "...I have married a wife, and therefore I cannot come."

To keep a balance in the test of the family, I must note that we are to be good husbands, wives, fathers and mothers. But if we are going to follow the Lord wherever He leads, we must put aside every weight and the Lord must be first, foremost, and only, not only for your sake, but also your family's sake. If your allegiance and commitment to the Lord is not clearly made known to your family, or they see inconsistency in your commitment, they can become a hindrance to your answering the call of the Lord on your life. If they understand your commitment to put God first and they see your faithfulness and consistency in following the Lord, then they will eventually join you in your commitment to answer the call of God.

2. Jericho - The Test of Our Devotion - 2 Kings 2:4

Jericho is the Hebrew word 'Yeriychoh,' which literally means fragrant, and it speaks to us concerning the 'devoted thing.'

There are many things in our lives that smell good to us, or things that we desire. Jericho was the first city that was to be possessed in the promise land. It was the first fruit and it belonged to the Lord. It was that which was Holy unto the Lord. Jericho also was the city that blocked the entrance into the Promised Land or the promises of God. It speaks of things that we are devoted to and have been for years. As Elisha did, we must go to Jericho and be tested in following the Lord in the things that we are devoted to.

The Lord must test us in these areas that we might be vessels of honor, fit for the Master's use. Our own ambitions, desires and things we are devoted to must be abandoned, and we must flee these youthful lusts (See 2 Timothy 2:20-22). Christ must be **all** to us. Our devotion must be absolutely to Him, and the call He has given to us. Paul said, "But what things were gain to me, those I counted loss for Christ. Yea doubtless, and I count all things but loss for the excellency of the knowledge of Christ Jesus my Lord: for whom I have suffered the loss of all things, and do count them but dung, that I may win Christ" (Philippians 3:7-8).

Let us put away our devoted things and commit ourselves to follow the Lord in the call He has given us, and let Him possess our possessions. Seek the Lord in prayer concerning this area.

3. Jordan - The Test of Denying Self
& Dying to the Old Man - 2 Kings 2:6

Jordan is the Hebrew word '**Yarden**,' which means 'descender.' It is from the root word '**yerad**,' which means 'to descend, or to go downwards, to fall, or bring down.' The English usage would be, 'to put down, put off, or subdue.'

This is one of the most critical areas where the final test of usefulness as a minister begins. It is the area of denying self, or to subdue yourself. In the gospel of John, Jesus said, "Verily, verily, I say unto you, Except a corn of wheat fall into the ground and die, it abideth alone: but if it die, it bringeth forth much fruit. He that loveth his life shall lose it; and he that hateth his life in this world shall keep it unto life eternal. If any man serve me, let him follow me; and where I am, there shall also my servant be: if any man serve Me, him will My Father honor" (John 12:24-26).

The final and ongoing test in ministry is to deny self, through the continual process of the cross. Paul said, "I die daily." He continued to say, "Always bearing about in the body the dying of the Lord Jesus, that the life also of Jesus might be made manifest in our body. For we which live are always delivered unto death for Jesus' sake, that the life of Jesus might be made manifest in our mortal flesh. So then death worketh in us, but life in you" (2 Corinthians 4:10-12).

Through the process of the cross, and the death of Christ working in us, to deliver us from self, divine resurrection life is imparted to us. It is out of resurrection life that ministry in Christ comes forth, ministry that manifests **THE MINISTER, Christ Jesus**. We must lay down our lives totally to the Lord. We must cross Jordan. Remember the blood of Jesus is for forgiveness of sin, but the cross of Jesus is for **deliverance from self**.

Even in the account of Elisha's crossing-over Jordan, he was actually laying his life on the line. There was possible death to himself by stepping out into the depths of Jordan.

Though the death process is ongoing, there is an initial point we reach in the process of the cross that qualifies us for the mantle of real ministry. I would term it an affirmation point.

Let us deny self and die to self, that we might live for Christ, and be True Ministers of Christ.

IMPARTATION BY ASSOCIATION

Starting with II Kings 2, the prophets stood afar off and "Elijah took his mantle (*the last thing*), and wrapped it together and smote the waters, and they were divided hither and thither, so that they went over on dry ground. And it came to pass, when they were gone over, that Elijah said unto Elisha, Ask what I shall do for thee..." (2 Kings 2:8-9). Elijah probably said, `You've gone all the way through the process; it's been ten long years. I'll tell you a few things. I've done everything I can to discourage you. You must really have a call because you haven't been discouraged yet. I've just about beat you with a baseball bat, stepped on you, stomped you in your face, and done everything I can to shake you off. You have a hold of the call of God. Now, what do you want?

"...Ask what I shall do for thee, before I be taken away from thee. And Elisha said, I pray thee, let a double portion of thy spirit be upon me" (Verse 9). Impartation is what he wanted; **impartation by association**. Whatever touches the holy things shall be holy (See Exodus 30:29). You produce seed after your own kind... (See Genesis 1:11-12). ...impartation by association.

In my own life, I have experienced impartation by association. I first started having similitudes *(spiritual pictures)* around Walter and Peggy Stanley who are a team used in an expression of ministry through similitudes. Similitudes are a part of the ministry that God has given me (See Hosea 12:10). I prophesy what I **see** many times. When I prophesy, many times I'm seeing exactly what I'm saying. I first started moving into this dimension of ministry when I was around Walter and Peggy Stanley and they were there to judge its authenticity, having been used in that realm.

I first began to move into the flow of the prophetic anointing after the late Brother Harold Moll laid his hands on me. A tremendous heat just ran up and down my body, and the first person I prophesied to, when I really knew what prophesying was all about, was Brother Moll. Even though I was crying and shaking, I went right on and prophesied. I was crying because I know that Brother Moll is a real prophet of God. He has been proven over the years. I was crying and shaking and everything. I mean I was scared, but if I hadn't given that word, I felt like I would have died!

That is what is meant by impartation by association, because when the flow of ministry comes forth, people that have been used in that particular office, or calling, are able to say, 'Yes, that's all right; that is the Lord. Be encouraged.' Or they might say that you're on the wrong track. There are people that know God's ways and can say, 'No, that's not it; you've missed it.' If you go down a continuous road of error, you may get so far out there that your ministry is no more. We have got to get you out of that state, just to save your soul and keep you from losing your inheritance.

It is good to receive from other ministries in the Body of Christ. John said, "A man can receive nothing, except it be given him from heaven." Other established ministries are an expression of Christ the Head in the Body. "Thou hast ascended on high, thou hast led captivity captive: Thou hast received gifts for men; yea, for the rebellious also, that the Lord God might dwell among them" (Psalm 68:18). The Lord has given people to the Church for its perfection. "And he gave some, Apostles; and some Prophets; and some Evangelists; and some Pastors and Teachers, for the **perfecting** of the saints for the **work of the ministry**, for the edifying of the Body of Christ" (Ephesians 4:11-12).

That which qualifies a person for real ministry is Christ, having imparted a measure of Himself to that person, to such a degree that he can minister to the Body for its perfection (See I Thessalonians 3:10). It is Christ deposited in a person and that person drawing Christ out of the Body. So impartation of Jesus

Christ Himself is the basis of ministry. But, we too must be willing to receive of the measure of Christ deposited in His other ministers.

Paul said, "For I long to see you, that I may **impart** unto you some spiritual gift, to the end ye may be established; That is that I may be comforted **together** with you by the **mutual faith** both of you and me" (Romans 1:11-12). Again, Paul states, "And I am **sure** that, when I come unto you, I shall come in the fullness of the blessing of the gospel of Christ" (Romans 15:29).

If we can't receive from one another, we disqualify the whole concept of ministry, which is serving, out of the measure Christ has given us. Be open to receive impartation by association (See I Thessalonians 2:13).

IF YOU SEE GOD

"And he said, Thou hast asked a hard thing: nevertheless, if thou see me when I am taken from thee, it shall be so unto thee: but if not, it shall not be so." (2 Kings 2:10)

Right when you are about ready to move forth into the anointing **to do**, you can find that there will always be things trying to divert you. You can expect it!   There will be many things to divert you, but it had been ten years for Elisha. After ten years, Elisha had not taken his eyes off of Elijah who had done everything he could to discourage Elisha. Elisha said, "Brother, you might as well forget it, I am not going to miss it now. There's not going to be any stopping here. I've gone through too much and I'm not going to waste my time. Elijah, I've been walking with you for ten years. I know how you eat. I know everything about you; I know how every nerve twitches. I know how you think and what your mannerisms are, God sent me here and I'm going to get it. I think I know you better than you know yourself."

"If thou see me..." The thing is he really couldn't see Elijah; he had to see God! If he had seen Elijah, he would have left a long time ago because Elijah said to him, `Get on away from here.' Brother, that is hard. `Get on away from here. What do I have to do with thee?' Elisha saw God! You have to see God! If God has set you in a place, you have to see Him, because you can get your eyes off center and miss Him. You can even see the person, and miss it. The person is not your worry. God has him in His hand. When God sends you to a place, He's going to keep the right person over you.

In a counseling session, I was telling someone, 'Do you know what makes me preach around here? The people whom God has sent.' I could not preach if it were not for the people that God has planted in the place where I pastor. As a result, God must grant unto me ministry that is going to bring the people to full maturity into that which He has called them. Impartation must come by association.

"And it came to pass, as they still went on, and talked (*Now he did not say dramatically, `Here it comes.' He kept on going in the regular conversation. You can think everything is just regular and you might miss it, if you're not spiritually alert and perceptive*), that, behold, **there appeared** a chariot of fire (*who wouldn't look at that?*), and horses of fire, and parted them both asunder..." (2 Kings 2:11).

That means that it came right in between them; it tried to separate them. Since Elisha was going to have a real anointing, he had to go through these things. He was going to get the double portion. He had to go through these things to be tested, if he was worthy of the anointing that was going to be granted to him. "...And Elijah went up by a whirlwind in heaven" (Verse 11). "And Elisha saw **it**, and he cried, My father, my father *(that was his father that we call the father in the gospel)*, the chariot of Israel, and the horsemen thereof. And he saw him no more: and he took hold of his own clothes, and rent them in two pieces *(humbling himself again)*. He took up also the mantle of Elijah that fell from him, and went back and stood by the bank of Jordan; And he took the mantle of Elijah that fell from him, and smote the waters, and said, Where **is** the LORD God of Elijah?" (Verses 12-14).

All the time he was not seeing Elijah. Who did he call on when he got the anointing? The **LORD God of Elijah**. The God behind Elijah is what he saw all the time. He had his eyes on the right thing, and when it came time for him to step forth with the anointing that was given to him **to do**, he did not call on Elijah. He knew the Source of Elijah! He asked, "Where is the LORD God of Elijah? He knew the anointing was there. Elijah was the vehicle God used to get Elisha to the place where there would be two times as many miracles as Elijah had done. "...And when he also had smitten the waters, they parted hither and thither: and Elisha went over. And when the sons of the prophets which **were** to view at Jericho **saw** him, they said, The spirit of Elijah doth rest on Elisha. And they came to meet him, and bowed themselves to the ground before him" (Verse 14-15).

The anointing speaks for itself. You don't have to work it up; the anointing speaks for itself. Let me give you another example, remembering it was ten years before he got **to do**.

CHAPTER 8

DAVID - TO BE AND TO DO

In looking at the calling of David, we refer to 1 Samuel 16. Samuel was told to go and anoint one of Jesse's sons king. His seven brothers came in. They were tall, dark and handsome. Then God had to give Samuel an illustrative lesson. Man looks on the outward appearance, but God looks on the heart. God was not interested in how they looked on the outside; that was all going to be covered up. When God puts his heavy garments on them, they are going to be covered up. The only thing that will come forth is what is in the heart. And then Samuel came across little ole' David.

> **"And Jesse sent and brought him in. Now he was ruddy, and withal of a beautiful countenance, and goodly to look to. And the LORD said, Arise, anoint him: for this is he. Then Samuel took the horn, and anointed him in the midst of his brethren: and the Spirit of the LORD came upon David from that day forward. So Samuel rose up, and went to Ramah" (1 Samuel 16:12-13).**

The Spirit came upon him and approximately seven years passed before David was fully active as an anointed king over Israel. While God's other anointed, King Saul, was chasing him, he could have acted in his own way. He went through a fast consecration period, constantly on the run. He was being prepared to wear the garments of the anointing. He was being made ready for the anointing to come and to **abide**! That is true ministry, when the anointing abides; then God can trust you to speak **His** oracles. He can trust you in any situation, because you have become an open hand. You've got the right words to say in any situation.

In counselling, I am amazed concerning some of the things that come up. Sometimes I believe I need to have a recorder with me in the counselling sessions. I would like for them to replay the tape and hear some of the things they say, and that are said to them by the Spirit of Counsel. We must desire to be an open hand, and that requires consecration. That is what ministry is all about, to be an open hand, to be able. Are you able? In **HIM** you are able. So the anointing came upon David, but it was seven years before he really began **to do**. That first anointing came to cause him **to be**. And David went through a lot of things and learned a lot of lessons. He became consecrated and he was made to sit as an anointed king.

> **"And the men of Judah came, and there they anointed David king over the house of Judah. And they told David, saying, That the men of Jabesh-gilead were they that buried Saul" (2 Samuel 2:4).**

This was seven years later after his first anointing that he began to reign, but actually the anointing came the day that the Word was spoken and the oil was poured on him. But it was the anointing that was given to get him right and cause him **to be** (See 2 Samuel 5:3).

KING SAUL - REJECTION OF THE ANOINTING

King Saul, though he was anointed king, never was **made**. His life-style never came up to the realm of the anointing; therefore, it was not only that the kingdom departed from him, but it was really the anointing **to be** king over God's Kingdom that departed. When you are called, the calling is there, but the enablement **to do** may not be there. I know folks that at one time had a vision of what God wanted to do in inner-cities across the country, but they didn't give in to it fully. Though they are still called, the anointing is at a low realm, because their life-style did not come up to that calling and anointing **to be**. They are not practicing a Godly life-style. Their flesh is showing. They wouldn't become fully robed in the garments of consecration, so now flesh is showing. The anointing cannot come upon flesh (See Exodus 30:32).

Though Saul was used in a measure, he did not get his life in line with that to which he had been called. He continually wanted to do his own thing and was disobedient and rebellious. It wasn't the kingdom that was taken away, because he was still king for awhile, but it was the **anointing to rule** the kingdom that was gone. It was the anointing to be king that left him: Therefore, he never came into an abiding anointing **to do**, because he had never been **made to be**.

BE YE CLEAN

"How beautiful on the mountain are the feet of him that bringeth good tidings, that publisheth peace; that bringeth good tidings of good, that publisheth salvation; that saith unto Zion, Thy God reigneth" (Isaiah 52:7). That is really a beautiful person. How beautiful **upon the mountain** are the feet of them that doeth such things.

Verse 8 speaks of 'Thy watchmen.' For many ministries are involved in a watchman's ministry, which involves looking unto God and looking out for the people. A watchman is one who sits high and sees what others don't see. They are God's chosen who are going to be entrusted with a lot of things that other people cannot be entrusted with. God's chosen are going to know firsthand what is happening in God's economy. When you're God's chosen, He will not hold anything back from you. He is going to let you know all things that concern your commission, and the things around you. You're a watchman. On a watchtower, you are going to see things that are far behind you, things that are around you, and even things that are ahead because you are on a higher level. God's watchmen have a good view (See Ezekiel 33).

"Thy watchmen shall lift up **the** voice; with the voice together shall they sing: for they shall see eye to eye, when the LORD shall bring again Zion" (Isaiah 52:8). Where is Zion? The place where His Presence is, where His praises are, and where His people are. Zion is a spiritual dimension of the Church. It is also a governmental realm of the Church.

It's an astonishing experience to go to another church and hear the same thing that was spoken at the church where you are planted. I mean sometimes the exact same scriptures are spoken. I used to just sit there and cry. It puts a reverential fear on me. It doesn't put as much fear on me now, as it did in earlier days of ministry, but I still recognize that it is really something to be caught up in the current of God. The watchmen shall see eye to eye.

It is when you come unto Zion that this begins to happen. It is not going to happen everywhere. It is where people are flowing in the realm of Mt. Zion. It is where God's praises are, it is where His Presence is, it is where His Word is and His ways are adhered to. Zion is the highest the Church is to reach in this dispensation. Many times it is exactly the same message. It doesn't matter where the minister comes from; it doesn't have to be the pastor of the church. They may be from out of town, but in Zion the watchmen see eye to eye.

God is saying the same thing everywhere. His Word is not something that you use to make up pretty sermons. God has something to say. He wants His Word heard and wherever people observe the Lordship of Jesus Christ, you are going to hear the same thing there. It is a blessing, and yet it is almost frightening. It really is frightening to know that God would entrust you with His very oracles, even His Word!

I remember one time I cried like a baby when we were over at a sister's house having a prayer meeting. When I went to church the next day, I cried and cried and had to run outside the place. Scripture, word for word of what was ministered at the prayer meeting was preached, and it brought a humbleness to my spirit. I said, 'Lord, we're tapping into Your current.' Now that is holy. You may not understand what I am trying to say, but it is holy. It brings a greater respect for God and His word when you know it is Him, in that type of situation. That is holy!

I have seen ministers in the church go out and minister at other places, and after listening to the tape, I hear the same thing that I've been preaching. Everybody expresses it in a different way, but it is the same thing God is saying. "Thy watchmen shall lift up the **voice**; with the voice together shall they sing: for they shall see eye to eye, when the LORD shall bring again Zion" (Verse 8). And, thank God, He has brought again Zion. "Break forth into joy, sing together, ye waste places of Jerusalem: for the LORD hath comforted his people, he hath redeemed Jerusalem. The LORD hath make bare His holy arm *(that means He is ready to move)* in the eyes of all the nations" (Verses 9-10).

He has rolled back that sleeve and made it bare. He is ready to do something! That is what He is doing with the Church right now. He is bringing the Church forth, in front of all the nations. He says, "I want you to see My Church! I'm preparing for My Church to begin to move; my instruments in the Earth to move, that I may show forth My glory and My power and make everybody obedient to the Word of God." He is ready to show His arm bare. He is ready to move in this hour. "The LORD hath made bare His holy arm in the eyes of all the nations; and all the ends of the earth shall see *(ALL the ends of the Earth shall see)* the salvation of our God." (Verse 10) Where are they going to see it? They are going to see the salvation in His people, those who have experienced and partaken of the salvation of God. "Depart ye, depart ye, go ye out from thence, touch no **unclean thing**; go ye out of the midst of her; **be ye clean**, that bear the vessels of the LORD" (Verse 11; underlining mine).

You that bear the ministry, be ye clean. If you know you are called, and you know you have had a Divine encounter with God and that He has touched your life and you are conscious that the anointing has come to consecrate you and to separate you, then **BE** ye clean, that bear the vessels or precious things of the LORD. "For ye shall not go out with haste, nor go by flight: for the LORD will go before you; and the God of Israel **will be** your reward. Behold, my servant shall deal prudently *(wisely)*, he shall be exalted and extolled, and be very high. As many were astonished at thee; his visage was so marred *(talking about*

Jesus) more than any man, and his form more than the sons of men... *(they won't see you)"* (Verses 12-14). "Be ye clean, that bear the vessels of the LORD."

And this is what happens at the beginning of a call from God. There has to be a consecration, and God must clean your life up. You are representing Him! Any business who hired you in a responsible position, they would be concerned about how you are dressed, and what you do, because you are representing them. When you go as a representative of a company, their first impression of you is how others see the company. How you act is how they see the company. If they see you sloppy, they are going to think the company is sloppy. What they see in you will reflect what people see in the company you represent. We are representatives of the LORD; we are ambassadors of Christ, but we are special ambassadors. (See II Corinthians 5:20) Everybody is an ambassador, but when you are called in a ministry, that is a special ambassador. To many foreign people, their opinion of America is based upon the ambassador who is sent to that country. That is why it is a matter of importance when we go, how we go, and what we do when we go. "Be ye clean, that bear the vessels of the LORD."

That is what the anointing with a call is doing, helping you to clean up your lives. And He will continue cleaning you up. What you might have been allowed to do for so long, after awhile even that can be sin, because you are constantly progressing, and your life-style must go up with the anointing; it must flow with the anointing.

"Nevertheless the foundation of God standeth sure, having this seal, the Lord knoweth them that are His. And, let every one that nameth the name of Christ depart from

iniquity. But in a great house there are not only vessels of gold and of silver, but also of wood and of Earth; and some to honor, and some to dishonor. If a man therefore purge himself from these (he is talking about the wood which speaks of flesh and the Earth), he shall be a vessel unto honor, sanctified, and meet for the Master's use, and prepared unto every good work"
(II Timothy 2:19-21).

"Be ye clean, that bear the vessels of the Lord. Flee also youthful lusts *(or desires)*..." (Verse 22). We have followed a lot of those young desires in our Christian life, that we find out are just empty. Get away from those things that you like to do out of a youthful passion and out of emotion. You must grow up. A mark of maturity is when you cease to be controlled by your emotions, and learn to reason things out, and look at things in relation to others as well as yourself. You must begin to consider the Lord and others in your decisions.

There is a time to play and a time not to play. Flee those youthful lusts and desires. Why? Because you are sent out and you are a special ambassador. God's hand is upon your life. You know it, and you have proclaimed it. "Flee also youthful lusts..." also means flee sin in its initial stages. Do you want to be God's chosen? Not just His called, but His chosen? **Then, be ye clean!** "...But follow after righteousness *(His character)*, faith, charity, peace *(His nature)*, **with them** that call on the Lord out of a 'pure' heart" (Verse 22). Change your company. All these things are involved in the call.

Some folks never know this, and after they are called, they just run. I see a lot of preachers preaching before they get chosen. They confess they are called, and that is as far as they go. Their lives and life-styles don't change.

"And the servant of the Lord must not strive..." (Verse 24). Do you know what happens when you strive? It slows the process of God, and it causes you to go in circles. As long as you are striving, God cannot say much to you. It is at a point of rest, waiting on Him, being entwined with Him like a braid, that God moves. And if He doesn't move, you don't move (See Isaiah 40:31; *the Hebrew meaning of 'wait' means to be entwined like a braid*). You must not strive to bring forth the ministry and your call. It will manifest itself. It can't help itself. "...But be gentle unto all men, apt to teach *(ready to teach and prepared to teach what you have learned)*, patient. In meekness instructing those that oppose themselves; if God peradventure will give them repentance to the acknowledging of the truth" (Verses 24,25). "Be ye clean, that bear the vessels of the Lord."

NOTES

CHAPTER 9

THE PROCESS OF CONSECRATION

The priesthood consecration is the most complete scriptural preparation for ministry. The priesthood was the first ministry God called. He called the prophets and He called Abraham, but as far as a **class** of people under an order, the priesthood was really the first ones who were called by God.

> **"And take thou unto thee Aaron thy brother and his sons with him** *(all these things that they went through are for a reason)*, **from among the children of Israel, that** *he* **may minister** *(notice the singular)* **unto me in the priest's office, even Aaron, Nadab and Abihu, Eleazar and Ithamar, Aaron's sons" (Exodus 28:1).**

There were **five** of them, and he referred to them as **one**! This is a picture of the five-fold ministry. "He gave some, apostles; some prophets; and some evangelists; and some, pastors and teachers" (Ephesians 4:11).

That is why he said, "Oh, you foolish, carnal Corinthians." For ye are yet carnal: for whereas there is among you envying, and strife, and divisions, are ye not carnal, and walk as men? For while one saith, I am of Paul; and another, I am of Apollos; are ye not carnal?" (1 Corinthians 3:3-4).

You can be moving in the gifts of the Spirit, you can be flowing in worship, you can have love there, but if there is envying, strife, and divisions, it is still carnal. There can be prophesying and the church can be carnal. It comes down to the individual, and if a church is filled with carnal individuals, it will be carnal. If there are divisions within the church, it is surely carnal, and God hates anyone who sows seeds of discord (Proverbs 6:16-19).

In Exodus 28:1, He referred to the **five** of them as **one**: "That **he** may minister unto me in the priest's office..." *(all five of them)*. That is a type of the five-fold ministry.

Paul said, what are you doing talking about Apollos or Cephas? "I am of Paul and I am of Christ?" They are all of Christ; they are all ministers of Christ. They are just used in different areas to help perfect you.

"And thou shalt make holy garments for Aaron thy brother *(for what?)* for glory and for beauty" (Exodus 28:2). God wants you to be a beautiful spectacle to the world; not in natural looks, but in the things of God. He wants to give you His glory that you might glorify Him in the Earth (See 2 Thessalonians 1:10-12).

"And thou shalt speak unto all that are wise hearted, whom I have filled with the spirit of wisdom, that they make Aaron's garments to consecrate him, that he may minister unto me in the priest's office. And these are the garments that they shall make; a breastplate, and an ephod, and a robe, and a broidered coat, a mitre, and a girdle: and they shall make holy garments for Aaron thy brother, and his sons, that he *(again singular)* may minister unto me in the priest's office" (Exodus 28:3-4).

The Scripture reads: Thou shalt make these garments to **consecrate** him. The word `consecrate' means-the act of setting apart anything or any person to the worship or service of God. And this is our aim in writing this book, to help you to separate yourself for the service God has called you for, that ministry can begin to come forth under the anointing **to do** because you have yielded to the anointing **to be** that came with your call.

Consecration also means to fill or be full of, or have wholly, God can't really fulfill His commission in you in entirety, if you don't give in to this process of consecration. He wants you to be filled fully with His enablement **to do**. Consecration is that process by which He brings us to a fullness where He has us wholly; that He can grant us the fullness of heaven's ability. Also, it means to fill, or be full of. To be full of what? To be full of God and His anointing or ability; be full of Him in what He has called us **to do**. It means to have **wholly**. It also means an **open one**. You're to be a hand and you're to be an open one. The Lord told Nathanael that there would be an open heaven and that he would see angels ascending and descending on the Son of man. Where is the Son of man? He is in you.

Through consecration, you become an open vessel that God can continually flow through and use. **A hand** is one of the meanings of consecration. You are set apart. It's a process of setting apart, and it never stops. You are continually being consecrated more and more. Your consecration moves into a greater realm, as God enlarges your commission. Consecration is being set apart, and coming to a place where you are full, and where you are wholly in the hand of the Lord. Revelations 2:1 tells us that He's got His ministers in His hand. He wants you in His hand. There comes a time where He says, `Humble yourself under the mighty hand of God that he may exalt you,' to become His hand.

There is a period of humbling and then there's a period of exaltation. What is He going to exalt? He's going to exalt Himself in you, through the calling, the commission and the ministry He has for you. He will exalt the ministry, if you will humble yourself and go through His process. Yes, there is a period where the hand of God is down on you, but there is a period where He has you, and you are **in** His hand, and He starts lifting you up, because you are lifting Him up (See 1 Peter 5:6; James 4:10).

Consecration means to be set apart, and an act of being set apart for **full** service, wholly belonging to Him; to be full of what God has told you to be to the point that you eat it, you drink it, sleep it, and it is a part of your being (See Acts 17:28). It must be to the point that whatever God has called you for, you're full of it. I'm up to my neck with God. A lot of people are up to their neck with other stuff, but it would be good if we were up to our neck with God. You're fully in His hand. That's consecration!

Consecration also means to be an **open hand**, one whom He can channel Himself through. That's the literal translation out of the Hebrew. It also means one given **power** and **direction**. It also means one that is able. **Consecration** is the ability to **be able**. Able **to do** what? Able to do whatever He tells you to do. Thus, that process of consecration is making you able. I'm able to do. That's why consecration is so important. An able one that has **direction**; in fact, the word means that when you are consecrated you actually **are** direction. "The path of the just is as the shining light, that shineth more and more until that perfect day" (Proverb 4:18).

Do all things without complaining, without murmuring, that you may be as light in the midst of a crooked and perverse generation that you may shine as lights (Philippians 2:14-15, paraphrased). You are **direction**! `As long as I am in the world, I am the light of the world,' Jesus said, `but when I am gone to the Father, you are the light of the world.' You are direction. You've become the way, because you have received **The Way**, and you are walking in The Way. So you become the way for others to come to Jesus. You are **direction**. You are **ability**. You are one who is **able**. You are **power**. In consecration, you become all those things and you become interwoven in Him. You no more exist out of yourself, but He begins to exist in you (See John 5:30).

What's a vessel? A vessel carries something. **Consecration** means that you become a **vessel** fit to carry the light and the power of the Gospel. It was important for the priests to be consecrated to the office that God had called them for. In the same way, it is important for you to be consecrated to the calling and the office that God has given you. I want to be full of what God has called me to do. God must be so real to you that he becomes flesh, or alive in you. As a result, you move in His presence at all times.

Consecration is an exciting word. It means to be full of the direction and desire of God. I remember when Brother Costa Deir said that he got on a plane and the man next to him asked him what he did for a living. Brother Costa Deir has a Ph.D. in psychology, and he didn't want to scare the man by saying he was a preacher, so he answered, "I'm a psychologist." The man said, `I've got some problems; let me tell you about them.' He thought he would get some free counselling. Brother Deir said, "I understand, brother, I've got all the answers. I really do." The man said, `What shall I do?' Brother Deir said:

`Brother, you need Jesus.' Then he led the man to the Lord and Brother Deir laid his hands on him and he got filled with the Holy Spirit on the airplane. The people on the plane didn't know what was happening when they began speaking in tongues. You should to be able to do anything that comes your way when you're God's anointed. **Consecration** means to be open at all times. No matter what the situation, you are ready. That's **consecration**!

Even though you might be called to a certain office, don't limit yourself. Even though you see a certain gift moving all the time in your life, and that's the gift God has granted to you, don't limit yourself. **Be an open hand**.

Sister Iverna Tompkins said, when going out to preach in certain places, they ask on questionnaires. She just says '**yes**.' They think she is too stupid to answer the questions, or all the answers to the questions are **yes**. 'I don't know how I'll be used,' Sister Iverna stated. Whatever the thing God wants me to do, that's my ministry. It won't be the same everywhere I go.' "What's your ministry?" The response is **yes**. I'm an **open hand**. It doesn't make any difference what your background is. It doesn't make any difference if you're called to be a prophet or teacher, you must be consecrated to do God's will. You'll surprise yourself every time you obey God, and do what He says.

BEARING THE BODY

"And Aaron shall bear the names of the children of Israel in the breastplate of judgment upon his heart..." (Exodus 28:29). Whenever you are called to the ministry, you bear the Body of Christ. In everything you do, there's a burden for the Body of Christ and there's a burden for the people of God, especially in the assembly where God has placed you. It's a burden you are ordained to carry. You bear the names of the children of Israel on the breastplate, upon your heart. When you're called to pastor, everyone of those people that God has sent to that church that He has planted there will be on your heart consistently. Whenever you pray, especially if you pray in the Spirit, you have got to pray for everyone that God has planted with you, because you bear them upon your heart. That's the burden you must carry. But God is really the carrier. He gives you the burden, and you react to it, and it keeps you in line with the channel of His will and His purposes. This is also true when God gives you a burden for a city, a nation, or a certain group of people.

"...Upon his heart, when he goeth in unto the holy place, for a memorial before the LORD continually" (Verse 29). As His chosen, you can have a little bit more of the expression of the deposit of Christ by God's grace (See Ephesians 3:7-8; 4:7). Everybody has access, but you're going to find yourself in a special place in the Lord. When you stand in God's presence, not only do you stand, but everyone that is involved in the commission that the Lord has given you, stands in His presence with you. There are people involved in inner-cities and urban areas all across the country, that we are to bear up before the Lord, because that is our commission.

The other day, I remember I was praying for the inner-city of Cincinnati. I don't know why; I just felt impressed of the Lord to pray that way. I know God heard it. Even though I had never been to Cincinnati, that's part of my commission. I'm as an ambassador sent to bear the burden of the inner-cities and urban areas of America and their spiritual state. You bear everything that affects the commission that you are involved in, and it continually broadens. It may not stop with your local

assembly, it may not stop with your community, but you bear
the burden of that commission. That is part of **real** ministry.
The Lord said concerning Paul, "...he is a chosen vessel unto
me, to **bear** my name before the Gentiles, and kings, and the
children of Israel" (Acts 9:15). Paul's burden was to a certain
group of people.

> **"...And they shall be upon Aaron's heart when he goes in
> before the Lord: and Aaron shall bear the judgment of
> the children of Israel upon his heart before the LORD
> continually" (Exodus 28:30b).**

That was Aaron's commission. But you bear your commission upon your heart before God all the time, and sometimes
the burden of it is such that you can't do anything but lay there
with it. But, remember, it is His yoke and He bears it with you,
and that makes it light (See Matthew 11:28-30). And, "The yoke is
destroyed because of the anointing" (Isaiah 10:27b).

CHAPTER 10

GARMENTS FOR MINISTRY

In Exodus 28, there is reference about the garments of priesthood. The scriptures are talking about Aaron's garments. The robe is an ephod of all blue, and the application is mostly for ministry. "...Thou shalt make **pomegranates** of blue, and of purple, and of scarlet, round about the hem thereof..." (Exodus 28:33). Pomegranates are a fruit so this speaks about fruit, or about nature and character. The fruit of the Spirit is love, joy, peace, longsuffering, goodness, gentleness, meekness, temperance and faith. That fruit has to be a part of your dress; a part of your covering. That is also a part of your consecration. Fruit is evidence of consecration and character. Jesus said, "Wherefore by their fruits ye shall know them" (Matthew 7:20).

"...Pomegranates of blue, and of purple, and of scarlet, round about the hem thereof..." (Exodus 28:33). Of course, **blue** speaks of **grace** and **divinity**. It speaks of **heavenly things**. **Purple** speaks of **royalty** and **mediatorship**. **Scarlet** speaks of the **blood** and **humanity** and **power**.

"...Round about the hem thereof; and **bells** of gold between them round about" (Verse 33). On your garments of consecration, there must not only be **fruit**, but there has to be some **power**. These bells are symbolic of the gifts of the Spirit. There has to be gifts or a demonstration of **power**. This also qualifies you for the office that God has called you to. It enables you to carry out your commission. But the pomegranates were in between the bells, and it kept the bells from clashing into each other. The pomegranates *(fruit)* also kept the tones of the bells distinctive and clear. Our message must also be distinctive and clear. "Yet I show you a more excellent way, and that way is **LOVE**" (See 1 Corinthians 12:31, 14:1).

The **fruit** balances the **gifts**. But they both have to be upon your garments. You have got to have both the **gifts of the Spirit** and the **fruit of the Spirit**. You can't have one without the other or you're not fully dressed, and you're not fully consecrated. These garments were the **consecration** of the priests. They had to be full of the dress that God had for them. This is concerning the priesthood garments, but spiritually, we must have the gifts and the fruit, one without the other means you're not fully dressed. God is a God of **power**. He's also a God of **character and nature**.

If I come into an assembly and hear an uncertain sound, who will go to battle if it's not motivated by love; if it's not mixed with joy, peace, longsuffering, gentleness, goodness, meekness, faith and temperance? When you've got the fruit of the Spirit and the Spirit is released in them, you don't need any law. Law comes when you don't have the fruit of Spirit in operation (See Galatians 5:23). That in itself is another study.

These fruit of the Spirit were in typology a part of the robe. Were all upon the robe. The linen garment speaks of righteousness *(character)* and the robe speaks specifically of office and dignity *(power and authority)*. "It shall be upon Aaron to minister, and his sound shall be heard when he goeth in unto the holy place before the LORD, and when he cometh out, that he die not" (Exodus 28:35).

You can actually end up losing your inheritance and God's best, if you're not clothed with the right garments. Paul says, "I keep my body under..." (1 Corinthians 9:27). Under, where? "I keep it under those garments." If you had seen the makeup of the priest with all those garments, you'd recognize that not much flesh could be seen. In fact, he had to have on linen breeches, which covered the bare flesh, before he put on the linen coat, robe, ephod, and breastplate. There wasn't anything that was going to show. I keep my body under God's clothing; under the consecrated garments which God has given me; under the blood. I keep my body under, lest after having preached, I **become** a castaway myself. You can be called, chosen and still end up losing out, because you didn't bring your life under the anointing granted to you with the call of God. You didn't bring your life under the authority of God.

As far as garments today, this could be associated with the admonishment that Paul made; "And that, knowing the time, that now it is high time to awake out of sleep: for now is our salvation nearer than when we believed. The night is far spent, the day is at hand: let us therefore cast off the works of darkness, and let us put on the armor of light. Let us walk honestly, as in the day; not in rioting and drunkenness, not in chambering and wantonness, not in strife and envying. But put ye on the Lord Jesus Christ, and make no provision for the flesh, to fulfill the lusts thereof" (Romans 13:11-14).

Part of your consecration is keeping your body under garments (See Exodus 29:29). God doesn't want to see you in your sinful state, neither does He want the people to see you in yourself only. He wants people to see what He has given you, and Christ within you. That's **real** ministry.

Those priestly garments were also woven in **gold** and **silver**. The thread was of fine gold. Did you know that the garments of the priesthood would probably cost a million dollars in today's market? That's a lot of money, but there is a price to pay for God to cover you up, consecrate you, and get you under, and it's quite a price. You didn't see anything of the men when the priests wore those garments except the head, the hand, and the feet *(and these three parts were consecrated by blood and oil, which you will understand in detail in the next section)*. The call was before them, and the people saw that they were consecrated and endowed with glory and beauty.

What did the consecration do? It covered them up. Do you know what consecration is for? It is for covering you up, or actually eliminating you and bringing Jesus forth. You don't want to die spiritually after having walked in the way of ministry. This greater judgement is because there is a greater judgment upon you, because you are called and chosen. Remember Moses and Aaron? One act of disobedience caused divine judgement. They didn't go in. They knew the way of salvation, but they couldn't go in to the promise land. He disobeyed God's commandment.

"And thou shalt make a plate of pure gold, and grave upon it like the engravings of a signet, HOLINESS TO THE LORD" (Exodus 28:36). This engravement is symbolic of the seal of God's character, that went on the priest's head. And we need the seal of God's character on our lives, above everything else.

THE BLOOD - THEN THE OIL

We will now deal with a further process of consecration that hasn't been covered pertaining to the head, hands, and feet of the priesthood. "And this is the thing that thou shalt do unto them to hallow them *(or make them holy)*, to minister unto Me in the priest's office..." (Exodus 29:1). "...and Aaron and his sons thou shalt bring unto the door of the tabernacle of the congregation and shall wash them with water" (Verse 4).

That is why the Lord sent you to the house of God, the physical expression of the church on a local scale, to be cleansed with the washing of water by the Word, that He might present to Himself a glorious church (See Ephesians 5:26). All the ministry in the Church must be in that glory too. "And thou shalt take the garments, and put upon Aaron the coat, and the robe of the ephod, and the ephod, the breastplate, and gird him with the curious girdle of the ephod. And thou shalt put the mitre upon his head and put the holy crown upon the mitre. Then shalt thou take the anointing oil, and pour it upon his head, and anoint him" (Exodus 29:5-7). They had to be consecrated first by having on the right clothing. Now, he is ready for the anointing **to do**! And until you are fully dressed, the anointing to fully move into what God has called you for, can't come.

You must be fully dressed. God has garments just for you. "And thou shalt bring his sons, and put coats upon them. And thou shalt gird them with girdles, Aaron and his sons, and put the bonnets upon them: and the priest's office shall be these for a perpetual statute: and thou shalt consecrate Aaron and his sons" (Exodus 29:8-9).

He can't grant you all His anointing with your flesh show-ing. Be still and let Him put His clothes on you. Then, when you come out, you're **really** going to come out. Don't be like John Mark who had to go back (See Acts 13:13). Some have gone out and have had to come back. When God sends you out, we don't want to see you coming back except with reports of victory. When Paul went out, all he came back with were reports of victory. Get fully clothed; That means fully conse-crated. From the breeches that covered the flesh to the linen coat, which speaks of purity, and righteousness to that robe, which speaks of office, authority and dignity, to the ephod, to the breastplate, the girdle, the bonnet, and finally the blood and the oil. All of it was a part of the priest's consecration.

The Blood: "And thou shalt take the other ram; and Aaron and his sons shall put their hands upon the head of the ram (*this was to identify with the ram*). Then shalt thou kill the ram, and take of his blood, and put it upon the tip of the **right ear of Aaron**, and upon the tip of the right ear of his sons, and upon the **thumb of their right hand**, and upon the **great toe** of their right foot, and sprinkle the blood upon the altar round about" (Exodus 29:19-20).

The blood upon your right ear is the cleansing of your thoughts and your hearing because our ears are our entrance into our mind. The blood puts a shield, a force field upon that hearing. You don't listen to all things, because they don't profit. It's to be upon your ear where the helmet of salvation should be covering our thoughts, cleansing our thoughts...purifying our way of thinking, our way of doing, and dealing with our personality. The hands, of course, had to be cleansed for service, and the walk has to be cleansed so that we don't walk in our ways. Some are willing to go through one or two processes, but they have to get that last one also. We must not take the things that we hear and the things God tells us to do, and go walk and do them in our own way. So there must be cleansing. "Be ye clean, that bear the vessels of the LORD" (Isaiah 52:11).

Many are called, but few are chosen *(being robed and chosen)*. Again, the blood covers. When the blood is applied, what do you see? You see the blood. And so we are talking about the hearing or the thinking, the service or the doing, and the walking in His way. The blood is the perfect humanity of Christ (See Leviticus 17:11).

Another application for the blood upon the tip of the right ear, the thumb of the right hand, and the big toe of the right foot can be looked at in light of **sacrifice**. For blood to have been made available, something had to be sacrificed. With blood being applied to the priest, he would be identifying with the sacrifices that he would have to receive. Blood on the right ear could be applied to the sacrificing of one's opinions and thoughts. As a minister, you have no right to have your own opinion. You must sacrifice your opinion for the opinion of the Lord. You must sacrifice your thoughts for the mind of Christ.

Blood on the right thumb can be applied to the sacrificing of our way of doing things concerning the Church and the Kingdom of God and being content to adjust oneself to the Lord's way of doing things.

Blood on the right big toe can be applied to the sacrificing of the place we want to go, the way we want to walk and committing ourself to walk His way. Looking at this process in the line of sacrifice would cause us to see that the priests were identified with the sacrifices they received. They were qualified to receive the sacrifices because **they too** were living sacrifices.

They had sacrificed their whole life, opinion, ways and walk to the service of the Lord. This is the principle in God's mind in Romans 12, which is a chapter dealing with ministry and offices.

> **"I beseech you therefore, brethren, by the mercies of God, that ye present your bodies a living sacrifice, holy, acceptable unto God, which is your reasonable service. And be not conformed to this world: but be ye transformed by the renewing of your mind, that ye may prove what is that good, and acceptable, and perfect, will of God" (Romans 12:1-2).**

See also, Philippians 2:5-8; II Corinthians 6:3-10; Matthew 26:39; Matthew 20:26-28).

> **"And thou shalt take of the blood that is upon the altar, and of the anointing oil, and sprinkle it upon Aaron, and upon his garments, and upon his sons, and upon the garments of his sons with him: and he shall be hallowed, and his garments, and his sons, and his sons' garments with him" (Exodus 23:21).**

All this is a part of consecration. He consecrates, then he anoints the consecration or the consecrated one. Sprinkling upon the garments deals not only with what you do, but what you **are**. In becoming anointed, the Lord takes you through a process of consecration. As a result, what comes forth is anointed. Not only what you **do** is anointed, but what you **are** is anointed.

Oil was sprinkled upon the garment, so that what you wear is consecrated for glory and beauty. And it is not only what you **do** that is anointed, but what you **become** is anointed as well. The anointing oil is not just to **do**; the anointing oil is upon you to **be**. That's ministry, when your whole being is anointed. Are you the anointed of the Lord?

The Book of Leviticus gives more explanation of the anointing of the priesthood. "Take Aaron and his sons with him, and the garments, and the anointing oil, and a bullock for the sin offering, and two rams, and a basket of unleavened bread; And gather thou all the congregation together unto the door of the tabernacle of the congregation" (Leviticus 8:2-3). "And Moses brought Aaron and his sons, and washed them with water" (Verse 6).

Sometimes some of us need a good washing. You will find yourself in the agitator more than anybody else because you are called. You are going to find yourself going through the washing machine of the Word more often, because others can do things that you can't do. Something you might do may be sin in your life, while it is not sin to someone else, because to whom much is given, much is required (See Luke 12:48). Remember that you are called.

Every once in awhile, when I'm preaching, I'll say something that is directed to the minister that is called to preach, and it may be a hard thing. Jesus didn't say everything to everyone. When He told the disciples, 'Except you deny mother, father, sister, and brother and wife and your own life, you cannot be My disciple,' He wasn't talking to everybody (See Luke 14:26). Many times He pulled His disciples aside and taught them a principle that was specifically for ministry.

"And he put upon him the coat, and girded him with the girdle..." (Verse 7) along with all the other garments. "And Moses took the anointing oil, and anointed the tabernacle and all that was therein, and sanctified them" (Verse 10). Know ye not that ye are the temple of the Holy Ghost (See 1 Corinthians 6:19)? God wants every part of your being to give way to the anointing; everything that affects your life to give way to the anointing. When all the garments are on, then sprinkle the oil. And that's the oil that seals what you **are** and enables you to **do**.

It was to be sprinkled upon the garments, but it was also to be poured upon the head. And remember that the oil is first poured on the head and then on the garments of the body. Jesus Christ is our Head, and the Church is His Body.

"...And anointed the tabernacle and all that was therein, and sanctified them *(set them apart)*. And he sprinkled thereof upon the altar seven times..." (Verses 10-11). The altar speaks of the **heart**. That's the main thing. He said, seven times, so that they were perfected in their heart. The number 7 is symbolic of perfection, completion, and fullness, as it relates to man. "For the eyes of the LORD run to and fro throughout the whole Earth, to shew Himself strong in the behalf of them whose heart is **perfect** toward Him..." (2 Chronicles 16:9).

The word `perfect' means full, complete, and whole. David prayed for Solomon to have a perfect heart and a willing mind (See 2 Chronicles 28:9). The Scripture says that they were to sprinkle the altar seven times. Make sure that the heart is perfect, because that's the seedbed of everything else. If there is not purity in heart, it is going to reflect in the garments and the rest of the clothing. Get that heart right. Sprinkle it seven times so you can make sure it's right (See Proverb 4:23).

You know what is involved with the heart? Motives and attitudes are where most of our problems lie. What is our motive in doing what we're doing? What is our attitude in saying something? You can do a thing and it looks all right on the outside, but your attitude and motives are just not right; therefore, God can't anoint it nor back it up.

As a result of going through the consecration process that God had for Aaron, notice what happened in the 9th Chapter of Leviticus. He had done everything God had told him to do in offerings and all the commandments. "And Aaron lifted up his hands toward the people, and blessed them, and came down from offering of the sin offering, and the burnt offering, and peace offerings. And Moses and Aaron went into the tabernacle of the congregation, and came out, and blessed the people: **and the glory of the LORD appeared unto all the people**" (Leviticus 9:22-23).

When you've gone through that process of cleansing and consecration, the glory of the Lord will appear in the ministry that He has called you to. "And there came a fire out from before the LORD *(and there will be a divine witness from heaven in everything you do)*, and consumed upon the altar the burnt offering and the fat: which when all the people saw, they shouted, and fell on their faces" (Leviticus 9:24). Not only will they fall on their faces, but they will respect your ministry. People will respect your ministry; they will know it is of God. God will **bring** His glory and **put** His glory **upon** your ministry and manifest His glory **in** your ministry. He will give a divine witness from heaven and the people will end up giving glory to God. And people will give ear to the ministry that God has called you to, because it is a real ministry, and a real ministry is God's ministry.

When you go through that process of consecration, you don't have to call yourself Reverend so and so; it will just show. You don't have to say, 'I'm a prophet,' or 'I'm an apostle.' It doesn't make any difference if you don't have a **title** in the called, consecrated, and chosen ministry, because it will show. The real glory will show. God will give a divine witness and the people will know it. There is no other way to come into anointed ministry. Any other way is the back door; it's the way of the thief and the robber.

It has to be His way. You need to be in a state where God can put **His glory** upon your ministry and continually give a divine witness of the call He has given you. Live in a state where He can give a witness from heaven, flowing in and through you as a result of what you do, and people will know it. You don't have to push it; you don't have to strive. They will know that you're a chosen one of the Lord, His called, His anointed. God will witness it. That's **real** ministry, **a ministry of Glory!** (See 2 Corinthians 3:6,8,18; 4:1)

THE HOLY ANOINTING OIL

In Exodus, Chapter 30, we see some things concerning the anointing oil. "And thou shall make it an oil of holy ointment, and ointment compound after the art of the apothecary: it shall be a holy anointing oil. And thou shall anoint the tabernacle of the congregation therewith, and the ark of the testimony, And the table and all his vessels, and the candlestick and his vessels *(everything had to be anointed)*, and the altar of incense, And the altar of burnt offering with all his vessels, and the laver and his foot. And thou shalt sanctify them, that they may be most holy: whatsoever toucheth them shall be holy" (Exodus 30:25-29).

When you go through the process of consecration, do you know what happens? God can grant to you a continual ministry of impartation. Whatever touches you gets what you've got. Remember in the story of King Saul, when Saul sent messengers to find David and Samuel, and when the messengers came in the presence of the company of the prophets, the spirit of prophecy was in the atmosphere. The spirit of prophecy gripped them and they **all** began to prophesy. First, Saul sent three messengers. Each one came and they were in the presence of the Word of God, the powerful Word of God spoken by the prophets, and they all prophesied. Then King Saul finally came, and the Word of God made him naked, and he stripped his clothes off, because he had on artificial clothing (See 1 Samuel 19:18-24 and Hebrews 4:12-13). In the same manner, Adam and Eve were covered with fig leaves. Man has been trying to cover himself with artificial clothing, but now God wants to put the **real** clothing upon you. God wants to clothe you! In the Book of Revelation, it says that Jesus was clothed to the feet (See Revelation 1:13).

Now, continuing with Saul and Samuel, in this atmosphere, they began to prophesy. That was the calling of Samuel and the prophets, and it touched everybody that was around them. God wants you to come to the place that when anybody comes around you, and touches you, they are touching something holy because you're not there alone. The Holy One of Israel surrounds you in the commission He has given you. If the garments and the clothing of God are surrounding you, they can't touch your flesh. You've got on all the proper garments and they are anointed. When they touch you, they touch God. Now, that's ministry. I'm talking about **real** ministry. It's not based on you; it's based on Him. God wants to cover you up, and bring Christ forth. Anything that touches you will be holy. That's the life of a true minister of God. What we call the anointing is really the action of the Anointed One.

"And thou shalt anoint Aaron and his sons, and consecrate them, that they may minister unto Me in the priest's office. And thou shalt speak unto the children of Israel,

saying, This shall be an holy anointing oil unto Me throughout your generations" (Exodus 30:30-31).

This anointing process also relates to us. They had to be anointed. They had a physical oil on them, which was nothing more than a symbol of the Holy Spirit and the power of the Word. "Upon man's flesh shall it not be poured, neither shall ye make any other like it, after the composition of it: it is holy, and it shall be holy unto you. Whosoever compoundeth any like it *(you know that people are really trying to imitate the Holy Ghost, and are trying to imitate the anointing)*, or whosoever putteth any of it upon a stranger, shall even be cut off from his people" (Exodus 30:32-33).

This passage of Scripture shows the importance of the anointing oil in the consecration of the priests, the kings, and the prophets of the Old Testament. When you are called, the anointing is also very important. It's important that you receive this. The anointing must be the final process of a consecrated minister. As you have on the proper garments for ministry, then the Lord can anoint you, and pour the oil upon your lives.

REJECTION OF THE PROCESS
OF CONSECRATION

In the 10th Chapter of Leviticus, Nadab and Abihu, the sons of Aaron went another way. As a result, they died. "And Nadab and Abihu, the sons of Aaron, took either of them his censer, and put fire therein, and put incense thereon, and offered strange fire before the LORD, which He commanded them not" (Leviticus 10:1). They weren't supposed to do that. They missed the consecration process. They tried to do it without God's seal. They weren't chosen for that; they didn't abide in their calling. They got a witness from heaven, but it was a **witness of judgment**. Notice in verse 5 that they were burned, but not the holy garments, because the garments were a part of their **consecration**, imparted to them by the Lord.

They took a censer and put fire therein and put incense thereon, and offered **strange fire**. Do you know what strange fire really means? They were **strangers** offering fire. It was false service, false worship, false ministry from **afar off**. I don't have any part with this fire. I have not approved of what you are doing. I don't know you. Depart from Me, I never knew you," says the Lord. Many said, 'I did this; I did that.' Jesus said, "Depart from Me, I never knew you" (See Matthew 7:21-23). Do you know who He knows? He knows His sons. God has fellowship with His Son (1 Corinthians 1:9), which involves His character, His nature. "You never walked in My ways; you never had My character and nature. You did your own thing. I don't know you. I know My Son. I don't see My Son in you." Paul said, "But when it pleased God, who separated me from my mother's womb, and called me by His grace, to **reveal His Son in me**, that I might preach Him..." (Galatians 1:15-16).

God can use a donkey if He has to, but He wants you identified with the anointing and the Anointed. He wants your life identified with what He has given you. Nadab and Abihu offered strange fire. They got a witness, but it was a witness that brought judgment. "And there went out fire from the LORD, and devoured them, and they died before the LORD" (Leviticus 10:2). The LORD said, "I don't want any pity party; I don't want any mourning. Aaron, don't you cry. Don't you bother with them." It seems like that was hard, but he had commanded them not to offer strange fire.

We are commanded to be clean vessels of the Lord! There must be a consecration. Since we know we are called, there has to be a separation, consecration and a cleansing to prepare us for the anointing to **do**.

NOTES

CHAPTER 11

THE ANOINTING THAT ABIDES

Now we are looking to come to a full ministry and a full anointing. Let's consider John's gospel: "And I knew Him not: but He that sent me to baptize with water, the same said unto me, Upon whom thou shalt see the Spirit descending, and **remaining** on Him, the same is He which baptizeth with the Holy Ghost" (John 1:33).

That is why we are being **made**, for the anointing to descend and **remain** that God can give the ability so that you are **well able** in any given situation to manifest the glory of God! The anointing remaining on Him was the thing that identified Him as the Lamb, the Christ. In the same capacity, we will be identified as Ministers of Christ when the anointing **remains** and **abides** in our lives and in our expression of ministry.

"The Spirit of the LORD God **is** upon me; because the LORD hath..." does it say, called me to preach? No, it says, "...**anointed** me to preach..." (Isaiah 61:1). The Spirit of the Lord is upon you because He has **anointed** you. This is in comparison, when David was anointed with oil, the Spirit of God came **upon** him from that day forward.

"...Anointed me to preach good tidings unto the meek; he hath sent me to bind up the brokenhearted, to proclaim liberty to the captives, and the opening of the prison to them that are bound; To proclaim the acceptable year of the LORD, and the day of vengeance of our God; to comfort all that mourn. To appoint unto them that mourn in Zion, to give unto them beauty for ashes, the oil of joy for mourning, the garment of praise for the spirit of heaviness; that they might be called trees of righteousness, the planting of the LORD, that he might be glorified. And they shall build the old wastes, they shall raise up the former desolations, and they shall repair the waste cities, the desolations of many generations. And strangers shall stand and feed your flocks, and the sons of the alien shall be your plowmen and your vinedressers. But ye shall be named the Priests of the LORD: men shall call you the Ministers of our God: ye shall eat the riches of the Gentiles, and in their glory shall ye boast yourselves *(there's some prosperity in that too)*. For your shame ye shall have double *(all these promises are involved in being anointed to preach)*: and for confusion they shall rejoice in their portion: therefore in their land they shall possess the double: everlasting joy shall be unto them."

(Isaiah 61:1-7)

These are promises for those anointed to preach. He said that everlasting joy shall be unto you, and you're going to have the riches of the Gentiles; you are going to rejoice in your portion. "For I the LORD love judgment, I hate robbery for burnt offering; and I will direct their work in truth, and I will make an everlasting covenant with them. And their seed shall be known among the Gentiles, and their offspring among the people: all that see them shall acknowledge them, that they are the seed **which** the LORD hath blessed. (*Again, these are promises for those **anointed***) I will greatly rejoice in the LORD, my soul shall be joyful in my God; for he hath **clothed** me with garments of salvation, he hath **covered** me with the robe of righteousness, as a bridegroom decked **himself** with ornaments, and as a bride adorneth **herself** with her jewels. For as the Earth bringeth forth her bud, and as the garden causeth the things that are sown in it to spring forth; so the Lord God will cause **righteousness** and **praise** to spring forth before all the **nation**" (Isaiah 61:8-11). All this will come to pass through the preaching of the gospel by anointed ministers.

> **"For Zion's sake will I not hold my peace, and for Jerusalem's sake I will not rest, until the righteousness thereof go forth as brightness, and the salvation thereof as a lamp that burneth. And the Gentiles shall see thy righteousness, and all kings thy glory; and thou shalt be called by a new name, which the mouth of the Lord shall name" (Isaiah 62:1-2).**

The Lord has called His ministers, anointed by Him, to show forth His righteousness and His glory. We are ministers of His glory!

He said that He will send you before all nations, didn't He? He shall reveal His arm before **all** nations. It is those who are anointed to preach. That word '**anointed**' in Isaiah 61:1 means 'to rub with oil.' It is not just a pouring on. He has to **anoint** you for your call and then rub it in so that when He pours the other anointing **to do** on you, the Anointed One will be revealed in you (See Galatians 1:15-16). **It is the anointing all the way through!**

When the anointing comes **to do**, all it is going to touch is more anointing! The anointing **to do** comes on those anointed **to be**. Do you know that when you paint something, you have to go over it? When you paint something, it changes the color; it looks new (See 2 Corinthians 5:17). The word '**anointing**' actually means to **paint**, to consecrate, to rub with oil. That is why the first anointing comes to get in your very being and every area of your life, so God can come and pour the anointing **to do** on you, and the anointing can remain, because it does not meet flesh. The Scripture says that the anointing oil could not come upon any flesh (See Exodus 30:32). Can you sense God rubbing the anointing in every area? The word '**anointing**' means to **rub in**, that is, covered completely with the Holy oil.

THE TEST OF THE ABIDING ANOINTING

In the gospel of Luke is an account when Jesus became ready for service. During this time, He was **being made** for ministry in His life. It was not time for it to come forth. Though the anointing was upon Him from birth *(He was birthed by the Holy Ghost)*, the anointing **to do** wasn't there yet. In Elisha's life before the anointing **to do** was there, we saw where Elisha was tested. "And Jesus being full of the Holy Ghost returned from Jordan *(notice that He returned from Jordan, a type of dying to self and it's ambition, just as Elisha had to do through the process of crossing Jordan before He moved into public ministry of His own)*, and was led by the Spirit into the wilderness" (Luke 4:1).

Remember that it was not Satan that led Jesus into the wilderness. Satan never led Jesus. The Holy Spirit led Jesus. And Jesus went into the wilderness, to be tempted in some areas in which God had to prepare Him for the last time, just like Elisha was checked out for the last time. The Spirit checked Jesus out. Would He do His own thing? Was He in His own ways? "If you are really the Son of God, it is no problem for you to turn this stone into bread," is an example (See Luke 4:3).

Will you act out of your own initiative? "I can do **nothing** of Myself." Jesus proved this statement (See John 5:19). God is going to test us when it is time for the **anointing to come and abide**. Will you only move when He says move, or will you do your own thing? If you have not come to that realm yet, it is not time for the anointing to remain. The anointing is there to **make you be**. Until the anointing brings you to the realm that you are nothing, and you become somebody that can do nothing of yourself, then the anointing **to do** cannot come.

The tests that Jesus went through are illustrative of some of the tests that ministers of Christ must go through in order for the **anointing to abide**. Would He operate outside of God, would He do His own thing? The enemy came to tempt Jesus first in His flesh, because He was hungry. Then the enemy tempted Jesus for glory and for fame: `Get up on this pinnacle. We'll take you up on this pinnacle so that You can fall down and the angels will take charge over you.' The pinnacle of the temple in Jerusalem was located in a place where people were always around in the courts. There were always crowds around the temple place. To fall down from there and not be hurt would give Him widespread fame and attention. `Oh, look at that guy.' Will you try to be seen and get fame?

This is a question that must be settled if you want the anointing to abide. The glory of men was the issue, and God had to allow Jesus to be tested in that area. What are your motives? Do you want to be seen? Do you want to bring glory to yourself?

And the last area Jesus was tempted in was His spirit, soul and body. He was tested in whom He would worship. The enemy took Jesus on a great mountain and showed Him all the glory of the world. That area touches not only the body, but everything that concerns you. "And Jesus answered and said unto him, Get thee behind me, Satan: for it is written, Thou shalt worship the Lord thy God, and him only shalt thou serve" (Luke 4:8).

As a minister, you must settle who you are going to serve and who you're going to worship. You will be tested in that choice. Jesus answered him with the Word of God; He did not give in to temptation. Now, you can expect to be tempted and tested in every one of those areas; the area of operating outside of God and doing your own thing. Are you trying to seek glory of men and be seen of men? Will you sell God out?

Will you take what God has given you and go and serve the world? Many have done so. One of Jesus' temptations was of fame and the last one was of power, your own power. All these things will I give you, riches and power, doing your own thing, wanting to be seen, lusting for power, just to make it simple. **Jesus passed the test!** His allegiance was to God, and God only.

"And when the devil had ended all the temptation, he departed from him for a season" (Luke 4:13). The devil departed just for a season (*which means, until an opportune time*), but he's always trying to get back around at you at every new level, and every new expression of your commission.

COMING FORTH IN THE ANOINTING

"And Jesus returned in the power of the Spirit into Galilee: and there went out a fame of him through all the region round about. And he taught in their synagogues, being glorified of all. And he came to Nazareth, where he had been brought up *(God always sends you to your own hometown to be a witness unto Him, and your own neighborhood, but He may not keep you there)* **and, as his custom was, he went into the synagogue on the**

sabbath day, and stood up for to read. And there was delivered unto him the book of the prophet Esaias. And when he had opened the book, he found the place where it was written, The Spirit of the Lord is upon me, because he hath anointed me to preach the gospel to the poor; he hath sent me to heal the brokenhearted, to preach deliverance to the captives, and recovering of sight to the blind, to set at liberty them that are bruised, To preach the acceptable year of the Lord" (Luke 14:14-19).

But the Word says that after He was tempted in all those points, He returned in the **power of the Spirit** into Galilee. That word **'power'** is translated **'dunamis,'** which means **to be able or possible.** What is the anointing? God's Divine Enablement, God's ability. You must minister according to the ability which is given by God; the ability that God gives (See 1 Peter 4:11). You can only minister in the level of the anointing He has given you. All those prophecies of confirmation you might receive are to **make** you where the **anointing may abide.** This also means that He came in a special miraculous power; a miracle in Himself. That word **'power'** means that you are actually a miracle yourself. Not only are you a worker of miracles, but you are a miracle yourself.

Jesus came to make any impossibility, possible. He came with the force of the Holy Spirit. The word **'anointing'** in the 18th verse, "...anointed Me to preach..." means in its Greek meaning that He has furnished Me with what is needed. That Greek word for **'anointed;** is **chrio. It means to furnish what is needed.** The Spirit of the Lord is upon me, because **he hath anointed me** or **furnished me with what is needed.** Why is the Spirit upon me? Because I am **furnished.** The Spirit moves where the anointing is. The Spirit moves where the vessel is able to take it. The Spirit of the Lord is upon me because He hath anointed me, because He hath furnished me with what is needed. And it also means that He hath furnished Me with what is needed through the idea of **contact**. By **contact**, I mean I've been dealt with by God. I've been in God's Presence and I have talked to God. He has been in my presence, and I have been in His Presence, and there has been impartation by association, based on **relationship**. "God who in sundry times and divers times taught and spake by the prophets *(or out of office)*, hath in this last day spoken unto us by and through, His Son *(which is based upon relationship)*" (Hebrews 1:1-2).

You have to be in contact to have intimate relationship. I've been consecrated because I have been dealt with by God. I have snuggled up to God. I have been in His Presence. I have remained in His Presence, and now **He has anointed me**. That is why the **anointing** is no long-distance thing. People go to Bible school who never establish any relationship with God, and they come out without any anointing. The anointing is based upon **contact**. Even when they pour the oil upon you in the Old Testament process, they have to touch you. Even when He puts the mantle on you, like Elijah did to Elisha, He has to touch you. It is based on **personal contact**. The Spirit of the Lord is upon me because He has furnished me with what I need because I've been with **HIM**.

That is the secret to **ministry, staying in contact** with God, in order for Him to consecrate you and make you, so that when the time comes you can say, `the Spirit of the Lord is upon me because **He hath anointed me to do, to speak, to say.**' Don't think more highly than you ought to think, but think according to the **ability** which **God giveth**. We are to prophesy according to the faith which **God giveth** (See Romans 12:3-6). We can do nothing except what God gives us (See John 3:27). It has to be in HIM. He gives us grace according to the measure of the gift of Christ (See Ephesians 4:7). To what measure we let the anointing be rubbed in `to be' then we can let the anointing be poured on `to do.'

As a living witness, I testify to you that it does not take a long time for God. When you are released, the anointing abides. You are still learning, but you are consistently **doing**, and you are involved in the commission. You are walking in the commission; but the commission is broadening, increasing and enlarging. It does not finish until you graduate to be with the Lord forever. There is no retirement in the service of the Lord. You just **refire**! He will continue to give you an enlargement of commission and consecrate you again for His purposes and grant the anointing. It keeps going on when you have determined in your heart to follow on to know Him (See Hosea 6:3). When you finish one thing, He will give you another thing to do. In the ministry, you don't retire when you are 65.

IN CONCLUSION

"And He gave some, apostles, and some, prophets; and some evangelists; and some, pastors and teachers" (Ephesians 4:11). There are apostles, prophets, evangelists, pastors and teachers reading this book. **He is making you that the anointing might come upon your lives and abide.** Make sure that everything in your life gets in line with the anointing that comes with the call. The most important thing is the anointing `to be,' then you will have no problem in getting the anointing `to do.'

Don't get the cart before the horse. Some want the anointing 'to do' before they partake of the anointing 'to be.' As a result, they are not fully equipped. In God's ministry, you ought to be fully equipped to meet any situation that comes your way, or to have the anointing of wisdom to get to someone in the Kingdom of God who can help you. That's **real ministry**! Get every garment on so flesh is hidden. It does not take a long time, if you are willing and obedient. God is waiting on somebody to yield, but most of the time there is that tearing down and breaking down that comes first. That process is so that He can get you to where you will finally yield to Him, in order for him to begin to make you (See Jeremiah 1:10).

Some have four years of school, yet with all that education and knowing the Bible very well, the enablement is not there. They cannot do a thing with their learning that brings forth Christ. They have been tickled in their ears, but their lives haven't been changed. Their preaching won't bring the garment of praise for the spirit of heaviness to others; their preaching won't bring comfort to those who mourn, because they haven't been comforted by the anointing **abiding** in their lives. It is the anointing '**to do**.'

Many preachers are still struggling, "How do I come into real ministry? How do I let the ministry come forth? How can I...? God has written it and we have all kinds of examples in the Scriptures. He has a way and He has a process. It is He who makes you and gives you the ability '**to do**.' All He wants you to do is bring your lives in subjection to the call of God that is on your lives. If you yield to the process of God, He will grant you the **anointing** '**to be**,' the **anointing** '**to do**,' and the **anointing** '**to remain**,' in the ministry to which He has called you. Then and only then will **The Minister, Jesus Christ** be manifested in the ministry of the called, chosen, and anointed of the Lord.

'To be **anointed**' is to allow **The Anointed One** (*Jesus Christ*) to come forth and be seen in your life and ministry, ultimately bringing Glory to God here on Earth. That is the essence of the **Call of God**!

Cassettes and Videos from Jefferson Edwards

Video Tapes

by Jefferson Edwards - $20.00 Each

JE102 The Truth That You Know Shall Make You Free!
JE103 Buy Wisdom- Sell It Not
JE104 The Burden of The Season
JE105 Bearing The Blessing
JE106 Ministry of An Apostle (part I $20.00 & II $20.00)
JE107 Warring For The Seed
JE108 Guard Against Defilement
JE109 The Five- Fold Ministry
JE110 The Need for Apostolic Fathers
JE111 Getting An Attitude For The Kingdom
JE112 Kingdom Life Equals Kingdom Giving   (part I & II $30.00)
JE113 Breaking Limitations and Controls
JE114 The Ascension Gift Ministries (part I & II $30.00)
JE115 Anointing To Release A Black Remnant
JE116 Scriptural Church Government (part I & II $40.00)
JE176 Taking Responsibility in Our Season
JE177 Paying the Price for your Season
JE178 Judgment of Oppression
JE179 Judgment brings Controversy

Audio Cassette Series

by Jefferson Edwards

Black Destiny I

JE118 Black Men Announce the Coming of the King- $15
JE119 The Black Eunuch Who Changed - $20
JE120 Attack on the Black Marriage - $15
JE121 Black Men of Might In Scripture - $15
JE122 Anointing To Release A Black Remnant Pt I, II - $40
JE123 The Destiny of the Ethiopian - $25
JE124 Restoration of the Black Male - $20
JE182 Chosen - Not Cursed

Change

JE125 Expecting the Supernatural - $30
JE126 Strange Gods - Hindrance to Inheritance - $35
JE127 Taking off the Mask - $15
JE128 Spirit of the World vs. Spirit of God - $60

Prophetic

JE129 Being a Prophetic People - $25
JE130 The Forerunning Ministry - $25
JE131 The Prophetic Truth of Solomon's Temple - $50
JE132 The Spirit of Elijah - $15

Purpose

JE133 Don't You Know You're Chosen - $15
JE134 God Given Purpose - $30
JE135 What is Life? - $15

Love

JE136 Challenge to Love - $10
JE137 First Love - First Works - $10
JE138 God's Purpose in A Love Relationship - $15

Spiritual Combat & Warfare

JE139 A New Wave to Take Us Over - $6
JE140 Casting Down Imaginations - $6
JE141 God's Strategy, It Don't Make Sense - $5
JE142 Learning To Deal With Spirits - $15
JE143 Melchizedek Style, War Threw Peace - $10
JE144 Military Strategy To Take The City, Pt. I, II - $25
JE145 Only the Man of Peace Can Fight in God's War - $5
JE146 Psalms 2 - Maintaining Your Position - $10
JE147 Strength to War - $10
JE148 Understanding Spirit - $50

Doctrinal

JE149 The Blood Covenant - $15
JE150 The Laying on of Hands - $60
JE151 Restoration of the Spirit of Grace - $15

Revelation Series

JE152 Authority in The Spiritual Realm - $6
JE153 See Christ Alive - $6

Testing

JE154 A House Is Not A House Until It's Tried - $25
JE155 Surviving A Crisis - $15
JE156 What Spirit Are You Of? - $10

Black Destiny II

JE157 Now is Our Time - $20
JE158 Truth Isn't Really What You Think - $10
JE159 Freedom From America's Bondage - $10
JE160 Freedom From False Sources - $10
JE161 For Such A Time As This - $10

Holy Spirit Ministry

JE162 A Personal Relationship With the Holy Spirit - $5
JE163 Knowing He, The Holy Spirit - $40
JE164 Relating to The Person of the Holy Spirit - $5

Instruction & Counsel

JE165 A Sure Foundation - No More Lies - $10
JE166 Can You Still Taste that the Lord is Good - $35
JE167 Detecting & Healing Spiritual Cancer in The Body - $20
JE168 Expecting to Receive from Heaven - $20
JE169 Kingdom Life-style = Kingdom Giving - $5
JE170 Pressing into the Kingdom of Heaven $25
JE171 Qualifications to Go Therefore - $35
JE172 The Balance of the Three Witnesses - $10
JE173 The Church is a Hospital Not a Rest Home - $25
JE174 Understanding Spirit - $30
JE175 Why are We Powerless - $2

To order call or write
Jeff Edwards Ministries International
P.O. Box 300873
Kansas City, MO 64130
1-816-353-6224 or 1-800-820-JEMI

OTHER BOOKS FROM
Pneuma Life Publishing

Chosen - Not Cursed   **$6.95**

by Jefferson Edwards

When his resentment and anger were flushed from his system, God began to show Jefferson Edwards the divine and significant purposes he has always had for the Black Race. The Lord has used him to help others, both black and white, to reappraise their attitudes toward themselves and others.

Liberated - No Longer Bound   **$6.95**

by Jefferson Edwards

The greatest threat to a racist society is a Black man who knows where he came from, where he's going, and that God is his source.

Satan has done a job on us in the past, but I have a vision of change. It is time to break the chains of dope, alcohol, anger and bitterness. It is time to stand up and be the mighty warriors God has called us to be.

It takes a real man to walk with God. It takes a real man to restore the family. Are you ready? Liberated - No Longer Bound will launch you into your God-given destiny. Your time is now!

The Call of God   **$7.95**

by Jefferson Edwards

Since I have been called to preach, Now What? Many sincere Christians are confused about their call to the ministry. Some are zealous and run ahead of their time and season of training and preparation while others are behind their time neglecting the gift of God within them. **The Call of God** gives practical instruction for pastors and leaders to refine and further develop their ministry and tips on how to nourish and develop others with God's Call to effectively proclaim the gospel of Christ.

The Flaming Sword   **$6.95**

by Tai Ikomi

Scripture memorization and meditation bring tremendous spiritual power, however many Christians find it to be an uphill task. Committing scriptures to memory will transform the mediocre Christian to a spiritual giant. This book will help you to become addicted to the powerful practice of scripture memorization and help you obtain the victory that you desire in every area of your life. The Flaming Sword is your pathway to spiritual growth and a more intimate relationship with God.

Opening the Front Door of Your Church   **$9.95**

by Dr. Leonard Lovett

A creative approach for small to medium churches who want to develop a more effective ministry. Did you know that 75% of churches in the United States have 150 attendance? Opening the Front Door of your Church is an insightful and creative approach to church development and expansion, especially for churches within the urban environment.

This is My Story $9.95

by Candi Staton

This is My Story is a touching autobiography about a gifted young child who rose from obscurity and poverty to stardom and wealth. With million-selling albums and a top-charting music career, came a life of heart-brokenness, loneliness and despair. This book will make you both cry and laugh as you witness one woman's search for success and love.

Single Life *A Celebration unto the Lord* $7.95

by Earl Johnson

The book gives a fresh light on practical issues such as coping with sexual desires, loneliness and preparation for future mate.

Written in a lively style, the author admonishes the singles to seek first the Kingdom of God and rest assured in God's promise to supply their needs.... including a life partner!

Another Look at Sex $4.95

by Charles Phillips

This book is undoubtedly a head turner and eye opener that will cause you to take another close look at sex. In this book, Charles Phillips openly addresses this seldom discussed subject and giver life-changing advice on sex to married couples and singles. If you have questions about sex, this is the book for you.

Beyond the Rivers of Ethiopia $6.95

by Dr. Mensa Otabil

Beyond the Rivers of Ethiopia is a powerful and revealing look into God's purpose for the Black Race. It gives scholastic yet simple answers to questions you have always had about the Black presence in the Bible. At the heart of this book is a challenge and call to the offspring of the children of Africa both on the continent and throughout the world to come to grips with their true identity as they go Beyond the Rivers of Ethiopia.

Four Laws of Productivity $7.95

by Dr. Mensa Otabil

The Four Laws of Productivity by Dr. Mensa Otabil will show you how to: Discover God's gift in you, develop the gift, and how to be truly productive in life. The principles revealed in this timely book will radically change your life.

The 1993 Trial on the Curse of Ham $6.95

by Wayne Perryman

For the past 300 years, many Western and European Scholars of Christianity have claimed that Ham, Noah's third son, and his black descendants were cursed, and "[Blacks] would forever be servants to others." Over 450 people attended this trial. It was the first time in over 3000 years that Ham had an opportunity to tell his side of the story and explain exactly what took place in the tent of his father, Noah. The evidence submitted by the defense on behalf of Ham and his descendants was so powerful that it shocked the audience and stunned the jury. Evidence presented by the Defense was supported by over 442 biblical references.

Know the Truth $9.95

by James Giles

This book is an exciting journey into the rich African cultural heritage. It reveals unheard legacies of founding church fathers, biblical contributions of

Ethiopia and other African countries, the technological advancement and innovations of early Africans and many other valuable gems of truth.

In this book, James Giles approaches Black achievement with much research and comprehension. This book is part of the reeducating of not only African-American people but people of all cultures. Now you can also *Know the Truth*.

Strategies for Saving the Next Generation $5.95
by Dave Burrows

This book will teach you how to start and effectively operate a vibrant youth ministry. This book is filled with practical tips and insight gained over a number of years working with young people from the street to the parks to the church. Dave Burrows offers the reader vital information that will produce results if carefully considered and adapted. Excellent for Pastors and Youth Pastor as well as youth workers and those involved with youth ministry.

The Church   A Mystery Revealed $7.95
by Turnel Nelson

Contrary to the popular and present image of the Church as a religious entity known as Christianity, God's purpose and intent for the Church is that it be an international embassy on earth that represents and manifest the policies, dictates and purposes of the Kingdom of God.

In this book, Pastor Turnel Nelson addresses and outlines some of the fundamental measures that need to be taken in order to revitalize the Church for 21st century evangelism and discipleship.

Come, Let Us Pray $6.95
by Emmette Weir

Are you satisfied with your prayer Life? Are you finding that your prayers are often dull, repetitive and lacking in spiritual power? Are you looking for ways to improve your relationship with God? Would you like to be able to pray more effectively? Then *Come, Let Us Pray* will help you in these areas and more. If you want to gain the maximum spiritual experience from your prayer life and enter into the very presence of God.

Leadership in the New Testament Church $7.95
by Earl D. Johnson

Leadership in the New Testament Church offers practical and applicable insight into the role of leadership in the present day church. In this book, the author explains the qualities that leaders must have, explores the interpersonal relationships between the leader and his staff, the leaders' influence in the church and society and how to handle conflicts that arise among leaders.

Becoming A Leader $9.95
by Myles Munroe

Within each of us lies the potential to be an effective leader. **Becoming A Leader** uncovers the secrets of dynamic leadership that will show you how to be a leader in your family, school, community, church and job.

Where ever you are or whatever you do in life, this book can help you inevitably become a leader. Remember it is never too late to become a leader. As in every tree there is a forest, so in every follower there is a leader.

Becoming A Leader Workbook $7.95
by Myles Munroe

Now you can activate your leadership potential through the *Becoming A*

Leader Workbook. This workbook has been designed to take you step by step through the leadership principles taught in Becoming A Leader. As you participate in the work studies in this workbook you will see the true leader inside you develop and grow into maturity. "Knowledge *with action produces results.*"

Mobilizing Human Resources $7.95
by Richard Pinder

Pastor Pinder gives an in-depth look at how to organize, motivate and deploy members of the body of Christ in a manner that produces maximum effect for your ministry. This book will assist you in organizing and motivating your 'troops' for effective and efficient ministry. It will also help the individual believer in recognizing their place in the body, using their God given abilities and talents to maximum effect.

The Minister's Topical Bible $14.95
by Derwin Stewart

The Minister's Topical Bible covers every aspect of the ministry providing quick and easy access to scriptures in a variety of ministry-related topics. This handy reference tool can be effectively used in leadership training, counseling, teaching, sermon preparation and personal study.

The Believer's Topical Bible
by Derwin Stewart

The Believers' Topical Bible covers every aspect of a Christian's relationship with God and man, providing biblical answers and solutions for all challenges. It is a quick, convenient, and thorough reference Bible that has been designed for use in personal devotions, and group bible studies. Over 3500 verses that are systematically organized under 240 topics, and is the largest devotional-topical Bible available in NIV and KJV.

New International Version $13.95   King James Version $12.95

The Layman's Guide to Counseling $8.95
by Susan Wallace

The increasing need for counseling has caused today's Christian leaders to become more sensitive to raise up lay-counselors to share this burden with them. Jesus' command is to *"set the captives free."* The Layman's guide to Counseling shows you how.

The Layman's guide to Counseling gives you the knowledge you need to counsel in advanced principles of Word-based counseling to equip you to be effective in your counseling ministry.

Available at your Local Bookstore or by contacting:

Pneuma Life Publishing
1-800-727-3218
1-805-837-2113
P.O. Box 10612,
Bakersfield, CA 93389-0612